Remembering, Father and me

Memoir of
Marlene Dee Gray Potoura

Copyright © Marlene dee Gray Potoura 2024

All rights reserved. No part of this book may be reproduced or transmitted in any form or by any means, electronic or mechanical, including photocopying, recording or by any information storage and retrieval system, without prior written permission of the Publisher below. The Australian Copyright Act 1968 allows one chapter only, or 10% of this book, whichever is the greater, to be photocopied by any educational institution for its educational purposes provided that the educational institution (or body that administers it) has given a copyright notice to the Copyright Agency (Australia) under the Act.

Paperback ISBN: 978-0-6459322-7-0

First Published in 2024 by

**First Nations Writers Festival International Limited
T/as First Nations Publishers**

A Registered Charity (ABN 79 655 932 979)

2/53 Junction St, Nowra NSW 2540, Australia
Phone: +61 491 851 353
Email: firstnationswritersfestival@gmail.com
Web: www.firstnationswritersfestival.org

FB: www.facebook.com/firstnationswritersfestival.com

Cover Design: Busybird Publishing
Typeset: Busybird Publishing
Line Edited: Anna Borzi AM 2024

Printed and bound in Australia by IngramSpark

This is a MEMOIR. To the best of my ability, I have re-created events, locales, people, and organisations from my memories of them. In order to maintain the anonymity of others, in some instances I have changed the names of individuals and places, and the details of events. I have also changed some identifying characteristics, such as physical descriptions, occupations, and places of residence.

To my children and their children.

Marlene Sahela Dee Gray Potoura

Dear father,
I will always be your daughter.

Nehemiah Gray Potoura
At Sopas Adventist Hospital in 1966.
(Photo credit: Marlene Kranz)

Prologue

This is a solitary whisper in the vast silence of a forgotten story, by many, but not me. I have kept this story for 33 years. Now is the time to share it.

No one's heartbeat syncs with the rhythm of these words, no one's breath mingles with the essence of my story. I am but a humble teacher, a mere speck in the web of existence. Within me, there is a world of sensory riches, a treasure trove of memories that bloom vivid and alive.

I recall the crisp scent of the *uhina* needles on my hands, the rotted *karahai* slimy underfoot as I wandered the untamed forests of the Orian valley. The gentle caress of the wind through the leaves, the symphony of bird songs that tingled the air with melody - these were the companions of my youth.

Our lands, cradled by the embrace of winding rivers and lush forest lands, held the legacy of my father's ancestry, his toil and his commitment to the land. Every tree, every stone whispered of his presence, of his steadfast devotion to our home, clan and tribal lands.

But the shadows of the 'Bougainville Crisis' cast a pall over our idyllic existence, shattering the tranquillity we once knew. In that dark hour, we lost more than just a father - we lost a guiding light, a pillar of strength and our connection to our lands.

The echoes of my grief still reverberate within me, a silent scream that I cannot bear to voice.

There were many horrible things that happened during the Bougainville Crisis. What I share here are the fondest memories of who I am and the special connection I still have with my father. The connection was deeply rooted by blood and spirituality.

Father and I could feel the tragedy before it happened.

Together, we shared a remarkable intuition that allowed us to intuit the impending tragedy before it unfolded. As I look back now, I am wiser in understanding human connections – focusing that the blood handed down to us by our parents, our forefathers and our ancestors is much more alive, than we take for granted.

I have realised the saying *blood is thicker than water*, is taken lightly.

Yet it is the root of my existence, from whence I came.

As you read, you will piece together how the simultaneous events unfolded and ended.

And so, I write these words onto paper, pondering on memories in remembrance of my father, for my children and my grandchildren to read and know, a brave and courageous man, who is their bloodline. For I may never find the courage to speak of my beloved father, to paint in words the essence of his being.

But through these pages, his spirit lives on, a flickering flame that I refuse to allow be extinguished by the passage of time.

This is the story of my father and me. The names I have mentioned of my family, extended families, and relatives are included to help piece together the puzzle and reconstruct the memory of my beloved father, who raised me to love our homeland.

In sharing my memoir, my goal is to offer a glimpse into the enduring and universal themes of love, loss, and resilience that echo through diverse cultures worldwide.

Through the storytelling of my father and me, I strive to build bridges with readers on a profound emotional level, emphasising the intense impact of memory and the path to healing.

It is also important to recognise the roots of values instilled by families who nurture their children in the steadfast love of Jesus Christ, our Lord and Saviour, I aim to convey the message that through Him, forgiveness is attainable, and that in the face of unimaginable losses, only God can serve as the ultimate judge.

CONTENTS

Prologue   iii

When Rifles Reign   2

1 Fondest memories of my childhood.   5

    My extended families   10
    School days   32
    School Teacher   49

2 War rages in Bougainville   62

    Father leaves for Rabaul (1991&1992)   63
    Beloved Papa (1993)   68
    Rest in peace, my Papa (1993 November)   85
    Saved by a black angel   89
    The tears of an orphan   92

Glossary   99

Dedicated to all Bougainvilleans who lost their loved ones during the war.

When Rifles Reign

Thus, embedded in my heart.
Dawn came as a curse.
Grandpa mist dragged them in;
not his fault though.
My awakening that stood still
For Rifles rule I saw!

Came hurdling at my door.
Sleepy eyed, I witnessed;
The nest I called home destroyed.
Ransacked to ashes and ruins.
Scattered, as I fled and escaped.
Rifles fired over my head.

Mother held daughters' hands
and wept, as the distance closed.
Father and sons bounded;
as they bled and cried.
'Leave my daughters be'
'Leave our mother be'
Rifles whacked them.

Brotherhood and colour
came all to nothingness.
Bloodlines and dynasties
disrespected and destroyed.
Love, respect and honour
erased by the power of rifles.

A long march you took
Beaten and disgraced.
No court, no magistrate, no judge;
Heard your case.
A man without summons
Sentenced by the mandate of rifles.

Two sons turned away
Their backs they gave you.
Not hate, not cowardess, not fear.
It was love, it was respect, it was admiration.
For blood was about to be shed
As rifles were raised and aimed.
For on the bridge you stood
Bravely, powerfully, peacefully.
A man sentenced without a hearing
A failed constitution, a failed court house.
A failed race, a failed lineage.
Rifles fired!

Gift of life ended!
Rolled over that bridge!
Like a criminal!
Like a murderer!
Like a convict!
Like a NOTHING!

Innocence; twice proven by Divine powers
By One Who Created! Magistrate!
By Only Life Giver! Judge!
Crocodiles mouths He shut!
Like lions of Daniel!
Rifles ruled; Creator is Ruler!

Now, you rest dear papa.
Laid in your own soil
Ground you walked on
Coloured like your skin
Land you loved and treasured
Home of your ancestors.
REST IN PEACE, BELOVED PAPA.

1
Fondest memories of my childhood.
'Our grandmothers laid the eggs'
From whence thou cometh?

I was born to Nehemiah Gray Potoura and Margaret Kumitoro Kauva. My father was born around 1934. He was the firstborn son of Kovou Popui and Potoura Karoia. This gives him the title of all land rights, both on his mother and father's side. He was from Oria village in the Wissai constituency of Buin District in South Bougainville. In our culture the land always goes to the male sons, but all sisters are treated with respect and land is always given to them.

Nehemiah was from the Kauo Clan. He was of the chief family on both his patrilineal and matrilineal sides. His mother Kavou was the sister of Tunu, the paramount chief, respected through all of Wissai, Bogisago, Pauluaku, Turutai, Rukauko and all other surrounding villages.

Chief Tunu had two sisters, Kovou and Koki and his only brother Billy, who was named after the first Solomon Islander Missionary who came to Oria to bring Christianity.

Nehemiah's father Potoura was the only son of Karoia, the line of landowners in Oria. Potoura has three sisters, Kukuma, Mevaki and Pinaua.

The exchange of marriage was common in our area back then. In the case of my patrilineal grandparents; Kovou married Potoura and Potoura's sister Kukuma, married Kovou's brother Tunu.

My mother, Margaret Kumitoro Kauva is the second born child of Kauva Moini and Roandi Anewa. Kauva was from Tugiogu in the Makis Constituency, and was of the Okoirahu clan, in South Bougainville.

In the late 1930s when Kauva was around sixteen years old, he left home and decided to seek his fortune. He travelled around the New

Guinea Islands and when he was about eighteen years old, World War 2 came to the Pacific Islands. He was a tall, well built, soft spoken good-looking man and was recruited as a NGR support (New Guinea Rifles). He escorted the allied forces through the rough mountainous terrain in the highlands of Papua New Guinea and was a brave and fearless soldier throughout the years war raged in Papua New Guinea.

When I was growing up, I heard about the numerous good deeds he performed during the time he was with the allied forces. I even wrote a childrens' short story based on real events that my grandfather encountered. You can read that story at the end of this memoir.

When the war was over, Kauva married Roandi from Yamme clan, in Nonambaro village, Watabung in the Daulo District, Eastern Highlands Province. They had nine children and my mother Margaret was born in 1950 and she is the second born in the Kauva family.

Margaret is a wonderful mother. She is a God fearing, spiritual woman who has prayed for me all these years. She is a trained teacher and a midwife, who has delivered many babies, especially during the Bougainville Crisis.

I have never heard her cuss or swear at us, her children. She is a hardworking productive woman, who has kept us, her children going through-out all these years. As the years have progressed, I have also progressed in the respect I have for my mother. Though I might not have been impressed with some of the things she had done, the years have mellowed my heart into appreciating her as my mother, who birthed and raised me.

Nehemiah was around three to four years old, when World War 2 came to Bougainville. His father Potoura, got very sick during that time and passed away and Kovou a young widow, fled into the mountains of Oria, with her son - my father - when the war ravaged South Bougainville.

When they were in the mountains, it was difficult to find food as there was a severe shortage.

A man, by the name of Tuure, who was from the other mountain village, heard about the plight of the people of Oria and came to visit them. He saw that they were indeed hungry and so he brought food and fed them, especially Kovou and her son. He looked after them, until the day they went back to the lowlands, where food was easier to find, as the land was familiar to them.

When I was about sixteen years old and was attending Kambubu Adventist High school, my father invited the man Tuure and he said thank you to him in cash and goods. He also gave him a piece of land in the lowlands along the Buin Arawa highway.

When the war was over, Kovou left Oria and went to marry a man named Puriala from Wisai area in the mountains and abandoned her son (just as my father told me). Pinaua, who was Potoura's younger sister, took care of Nehemiah for a while and then he was left in the care of Billy, Kovou's younger brother.

So, Billy became a surrogate father to Nehemiah and brought him up with the help of his wife Kaulasi.

My father was very poor, when he was growing up. A boy abandoned by his mother and whose biological father was dead, can be quite a target for bullying and mistreatment. But his uncle Billy was kind to him and took good care of him by feeding him and giving him a place to sleep.

I wrote a short children's story based on one of my father's experiences, when he was growing up. The names are fake and I creatively set it out so that it can illustrate a lesson to young readers and also older ones. If one reads it critically, a good Christian lesson can be drawn out of it.

I didn't write that story to offend any of my people in Oria. It is a story to show the hardship an orphan boy goes through, when he is growing up. The names in the story are common South Bougainvillean names and do not point to any person in particular. The story is titled 'The tears of an orphan' and you can read it at the end of this memoir.

Nehemiah went to Irinioku area school, to do his primary education. It was quite a long distance from Oria and all other students also left their villages to attend the school. This school was not like the ones we see these days, because at that school, it was the survival of the fittest. Students who were attending that school were left to fend for themselves by looking for food and cooking the food themselves as well. Many parents were faithful in climbing the mountains and long tiring roads to bring food to their children, but my father didn't really have anyone to bring him food, so he fended for himself by hunting birds in the bushes, fishing in the rivers and making gardens. He was an excellent hunter and fisherman and other students respected him for his skills.

My uncle Jacob once told me, 'Your father used to swim to the crocodiles when they were sleeping and tie ropes around them. Then he would tie the end of the rope to a tree on the banks of the river. Then we would all wait for the crocodiles to wake up and thrash around, realising that they couldn't move.'

My father was a fearless brave man, with a kind heart. I believe that was how he won my mother there at Irinioku.

I heard a story about an Aunt, who was my mother's close friend when they were at Irinioku; this Aunt got possessed by a supernatural power and was thrown into the depths of the river Moloana into a pool under the walls of the cliff forming a cave. Everyone was petrified so my father dived with a torch and pulled her out.

My mother's cousin Engenamo from Nonambaro was married to a man named Naisy, who was from Oria. Most times, mother would follow the students from Oria to go and see her cousin, Engenamo. Once, when they were walking back to Irinioku with all the garden food they had to carry, mother couldn't climb Mt Sansaro. This is because the load she was carrying was too heavy and she was struggling. She was about to cry, realising she couldn't walk any further, when suddenly my father came and lifted the load off her and carried it all the way to Irinioku. Margaret walked to Irinioku with a smile on her face.

From Irinioku, Nehemiah and Margaret both went to Rumba SDA Central School in Central Bougainville.

This time, South Bougainville was quite far, but one good thing was that the local people were kind and continued to feed the students who came from afar.

Nehemiah, his relatives and friends who were at Rumba, made gardens again and built garden houses and continued to survive for the sake of an education.

While at Rumba, my father used to climb trees which had parrot nests and brought the whole nests down with their hairless fat babies and roasted them over open fires as they sizzled juicily over the flames and then eat them with cooked kaukaus or bananas.

He still went fishing in the rivers, but because he was now in a different district, he only fished where they were allowed, which was next to the school. He didn't go beyond boundaries.

While at Rumba, my father and mother's friendship blossomed into a serious relationship and it was quite hard when they went their different ways in 1965 to attend different educational institutions.

Margaret went on to Jones Missionary College in East New Britain to train as a primary school teacher and Nehemiah went on to Sopas Adventist Hospital to train as a Health Officer and Laboratory Technician.

In January 1969, Nehemiah and Margaret were married by Pastor Peli, who was from the Solomon Islands.

My extended families

I was born at Tabago Health Centre in Buin, South Bougainville in 1970, on the 11th of February. My father Nehemiah named me Marlene, after Marlene Broad, who is now Marlene Kranz.

Marlene Broad was a nursing sister from New Zealand, a committed Seventh Day Adventist who was my father's close friend when they worked together at Sopas Adventist Hospital in the late sixties.

Over time I would receive so many gifts through postal mail from my namesake in New Zealand. One that I still treasure in my memory was a pocket Bible, a KJV, that had a zipper. I tell you, no one in my village had that type of Bible in the late 1970s. It was the first ever and during that time, I still hadn't learned to read. That Bible stayed with me for so many years until I learnt to read when I was actually in grade three, I believe.

I also remembered a little fond memory, a story that when I was born, my matrilineal grandmother Roandi Kauva, came to visit me and she placed a hibiscus flower over my right ear. Both grandparents on my father and mother's sides were proud. I was their first granddaughter and throughout my upbringing, they contributed immensely.

I grew up in Oria village in our little hamlet separated from the Oria house line, by the famous trench that was dug across the main road. I believe this trench is long gone, but in those days, it was the landmark between Oria and Nakomai.

I was well cared for like a true firstborn princess. My aunties, my father's sister Namina and her Pinaua babysat for me, while my mother Margaret taught at Tururai Area school.

I grew up surrounded by my uncles, aunties, cousins, bubus and many relatives. From all my uncles, I always remembered my father's only brother, Ue, with so much love and affection. He was born after my father and he used to carry me up on his shoulders and right up against his muscular chest. He was truly my favourite uncle. I always felt this secureness with him, since I was a baby. I have missed him so much too, because he passed on with a liver problem when I was in college.

I roamed the bushlands of Oria freely, like a true jungle trouper. I hung out a lot with my cousin Sevina, daughter of my uncle Apuio, who is my father's first cousin. Apuio is the son of chief Tunu, my father's uncle, who was his mother Kovou's big brother. I played with Sevina, but she didn't walk on the ground for the first five years of her life. We sat on the kariani, attended by our aunties and we played. Sevina didn't touch dirt or play on it, because she was on a special initiation journey for the first born of chief children during the early years of her life.

As I grew up, I noticed a long scar across my left cheek and asked my mother if they were trying to make torohuis on my face. My mother told me that I was near fatally attacked by a hen with chicks. She related to me that when I was about 2 to 3 years old, we were at church on a Saturday and mother took me outside to sit under the shade of a guava tree. A hen was nearby with her yellow chicks and as I gleefully ran around, I raced over to the hen and picked up one of her chicks and she attacked me with her claws, nearly ripping my eye out.

The long scar looks like the tribal tattoos known as the torohui that women from Oria and surrounding villages cut on their cheeks. They would use thin fine bamboos to make the tattoos on their faces. Three long streaks on each cheek. I only have one long streak on my left cheek and it looks like our tribal tattoos.

When I was around between 4 to 5 years old, I went into the kitchen, as I was so thirsty from playing in the hot sun, and lifted a kerosene container and drank it thinking it was water. My father Nehemiah saved me with the knowledge received during training at Sopas Adventist Hospital, about Home Nursing and the treatment of swallowed poison. I have always believed that I should have died, but it was God's Grace that intervened and saved me, in a truly miraculous turn, where I was given my life back to live it in its fullness.

Mother told me that it happened on a Sunday, when Bougair or Cessna planes took a break from flying around Bougainville. On that

Sunday, when I had drunk kerosene, it was around 10 or 11 am and as soon as father took care of me by forbidding eating or drinking and he carried me around, to help me remain calm. Mother told me she prayed for a miracle and Father God in Heaven, sent a plane to land in Oria airport around 3pm and I was taken to Buin hospital. The plane landed there to drop off chartered goods that were not taken on Friday or something like that. But this story always warms my heart that there are miracles happening every day, everywhere around the world.

I also scampered along the Pauhu, Pirasi and Wuloli rivers with my uncle Donald Kauva. Donald was my mother's brother, the youngest in her family and he is only a few years older than me. When he was quite young, father and mother kind of adopted him and we grow up together. He used to take me fishing and I would collect the fish and pull the bush rope through their fishy throats before I kept following him.

I remember those times, we'd arrive home late and my mother Margaret would belt us, especially her brother. What I didn't understand back then was that after she belted us, she would clean all our hard catch for the day, then she fried them into crispy golden browns, salted them and then we would enjoy them.

My cousin Margaret Kiatui, my mother's namesake was another of my best friends, may her beautiful soul rest in peace. We'd carry the pots blackened by the fires and go down to the river Pauhu and scrub them with sand and leaves. Our little hands would get all sooty and black, then we'd wash them off with coconut shreds. Margaret and I were really close friends, all the way through to womanhood. Now my dear cousin Margaret is long gone and as I write and mention her name, my heart pains and yearns for her, with an unconditional tie that bonded us as we came out of those wombs and became great pals, a friendship that God allowed, right from the very start of our lives. But she encountered illness along the way and left early to rest.

There was also Katherine, a bossy and overly caring cousin, who dragged me through the bushes doing all sorts of explorations. We went looking for snails and cut down wild banana trees and collected snails from their huge leaves. We peeped under the '*mandai* trees' leaves and collected the big green snails. Then we went home, boiled the snails in salted water in large tins and then used a sharp prickle from the lemon tree to pull out their bodies, then washed them thoroughly and dried them in the sun.

After we collected assorted shells from the bushes and jungles of Oria, my father Nehemiah packed them in a box and sent them to Port Moresby. After a while, a thick brown envelope was sent to father. He opened it and saw another long slim paper inside. He took it to the bank in Arawa and then when he returned, we were both given K10.00 each. During those times, in the late '70s, K10.00 was like a K100.00. Katherine and I were very proud little girls, who got paid from Port Moresby for collecting snails. That was truly something.

I once climbed a coconut tree and slid all the way down and severely peeled off the skinny sides of my thighs and sat at my home for a week. But that didn't stop me from all the climbing I did, as I was a typical village kid, always climbing trees for coconuts as part of my everyday village adventures.

One thing that I can still feel and miss terribly, was the freedom, peace, love and everyday direction of adventure that seemed to lurk or hovered over our heads when we were kids. I roamed around the rivers fishing, picnicking, swimming and sometimes just looking at the beautiful scenery of the forest lands – beholding the lofty trees, the variety of vines and plants and the sereneness of the bushlands was truly breathtaking. The stillness was truly holy and still as a grown woman, I can feel what it felt like growing up in the beautiful Orian valley of pristine clear rivers and lush bushlands.

The scenery of trees, plants and the bushlands was breathtaking, the rivers were so divinely fresh and precious, and the birds, animals and creatures of the jungle were not dangerous at all; maybe a few weaning wild pigs, but overall, growing up in Oria was a luxury, for which I truly thank my father and all the land he owned.

I remember my father's aunty and uncle, Lukumi and Kuriu, who lived beside the rushing crystal-clear river Aibia. I can still feel the thrill I felt whenever, we were allowed to visit them and swim in the Aibia River.

Attending Church for worship was part of my upbringing and it was a morning and evening thing. On Friday, we'd all help our parents to cook and prepare food for the Sabbath. Then we rested on the Sabbath Day and attended worship in the village church, right in the centre of Oria village.

I was a pretty good kid when I was growing up and maybe once in a while fought with my cousins over playing marbles, but overall, we played house and built around the edge of Nakomai hamlet, strange huts made with leaves and wild banana fibre. We played hide and seek and sang weird songs while hanging on those Tamarara trees, that grew on the sides of the Oria Airstrip.

My Uncle Mosina, Katherine's father drove the tractor that cut the grass on the airstrip. Katherine and I would sit on the tractor, next to Papa Mosina and took those long rides up and down the airstrip. It was awesome back in the day, late 70s, but now, I look back and say, geez, we were so dumb then. Yes, the sun was hot and the Airstrip was like two football fields doubled in length, I guess.

During those days, there was no highway to Oria. The highway stopped at the other side of the Loluai river and the road via Panguna Buin highway stopped at Turutai village. Oria was isolated, so the tractor rides were truly a treat for Katherine and I.

How the tractor got to Oria was that it was carried by the Oria and Paghui people over the Sansaro mountain pass from Turutai, when it was transported from Buin town. My people are very strong headed and hardworking.

The DPI (Department of Primary Industry) borrowed a hectare of land from my father, right next to the Airstrip and they built two permanent houses, with showers, toilets and kitchens inside and tanks outside. They were very nice houses and they transported all the building materials through charters on BougAir. They sent their first DPI officer, Andrew, from Siwai to come and carry out experiments in planting new kinds of vegetables on the plot of land next to the two houses. Andrew was a regular guest in our home in the evenings. He came for dinner and talked about farming methods with father, as we listened in awe.

Our parents told us not to go near the houses or the plot of land, as DPI was doing experiments and they didn't want kids hovering around the plot of land and destroying plants that they had brought from afar to see if they would grow in Oria.

We were a curious bunch of kids, up to no good. Katherine and I crawled through the fence and checked out the garden, while Andrew had gone to other plots of land in the neighbouring villages. We saw funny looking plants; the cucumbers were dark green, almost black with bumps on them and the eggplants were yellow. We pulled out one of the weird looking weeds and realised that it was that orangey crunchy thing that Andrew was eating raw and gave two to us to taste. He told us that they were called carrots.

We kept going back through the fence stealing those carrots, until Andrew made it known to my father that the carrots in the plot were disappearing and he was seeing many little feet in the plot. My father asked me, who was doing that and I owned up and told him that it was Katherine and I. We got a hiding and as we cried under the guava tree, Katherine turned around and wacked me in the face and then we were both fighting on the grass. We got another worse beating and refrained from visiting Andrew's plot of land, but the yearning for a crunchy carrot never went away for me. These days, I am blessed that I live in Port Moresby and eat a crunchy carrot anytime I want and poor cousin Katherine, sometimes I wonder if she still remembers?

Katherine, we call her Kaida, and I were always out in the forest lands looking for fun. One of our favourite pastimes was cutting vines that grew on trees and swinging over the cliff or over a pool of water on them. This was great fun, and we used to spend hours on end swinging on vines. I remember a time; I swung off over the cliff and fell in the cluster of wild banana trees and luckily, I was not hurt. We also swung across river pools we built with stones and wild bananas and then would splash into the pool yelling at the top of our voices. These were the greatest times of my life and I can still feel the adrenaline of how excited I was.

We picnicked along the lush pristine Pirasi and Aibia rivers. I can still visualise how beautiful the river banks were with breathtaking crystal-clear mini waterfalls and springs. We would swim and spend the whole day enjoying the crystal-clear waters and drying ourselves on the smooth flat stones. Then as the sun sat in the horizon, we would walk back home through the dark forest land as the fireflies came out twinkling. As we neared the village, someone would yell out that a ghost was following us and then we would yodel and scream all the way to the village, where for most of us, the guava twig awaited us. After the twig was turned to smithereens on our legs, we would cry and eat our dinner in silence. Then we would be out and about in the forests again, digging wild yams, climbing galip trees, pulling down green coconuts, then end up picnicking again until we would arrive home late; guava twig again – slap slap slap - but we never learnt. I was a tough forest-trampling young child growing up in the 70s.

We would sit around fires in one of our bubus auluis and listen to great tales orated by our grandparents or aunties. One of the legends, I remember from my mamo, was the one about Kutuke, a creature who lived in the caves. During continuous rainy seasons, this creature would be heard moaning under houses or around auluis in the darkness, for the want of a piece of firewood. When it got hold of a piece of burning wood, it would tie it on its tail and went off into its cave.

My aunty Aretai's (may her beautiful soul rest in peace) stories were about witches. She told me the story about Kuipanana, a witch who stole infants. Her right foot was chopped off and it was like a stump and she would stomp it on the ground, if she was coming for the infant and sing *Kuipanana, Kuipanana*. It was really scary, how Aunty used to narrate it. One other was about two girls who went around the grasslands looking for grasshoppers and ended up in a dark forest and saw a house at the edge of a cliff. When they entered the house, they saw smoked bodies of children on the tava.

I must say, these stories used to scare me senseless!

But the weirdest stories were told by Wamo. Now Wamo, was a hunchback, with unbelievable tales and he was a relation of my mamo's sister's husband. He was from Bogisago, in the mountains, and we would look forward to his visits because he would tell us the most unbelievable tales. Reflecting on his stories, I can't help but chuckle at our youthful naivety.

The tales that captivated us as children would hardly pass muster with today's discerning youth. He once spun a tale of a mistreated widow who passed away during pregnancy. In a macabre twist of fate, her child was born posthumously in the grave, subsisting in a manner most unnatural until he emerged, making his way back to the village. It seems almost extraterrestrial now, but Wamo had a gift for storytelling. May he rest in peace; his return to the village was marked by tragedy, as he succumbed to epilepsy while swimming. In our dialect, people with epilepsy are known as 'kurupaho.'

Our nights were spent listening to tales. We would have turns sharing a story but mostly, it was the old people who would tell us stories orated through generations.

Aloysius, my uncle's brother-in-law who came to live with us and attend Hairu primary school was a great story teller. He would tell us stories about his very own brother in-law, who married his sister and who he totally disliked because the man was lazy and unproductive. He nicknamed him Tuha and told us tales of how lazy the man was. My whole family would sit down after a meal and listen to Aloysius relating stories of what a failure his brother in-law was. He recounted the stories in a humorous way and all of us would end up laughing after he finished.

Apart from badmouthing his brother in-law, Aloysius also told us unbelievable tales. One I still remember was about Induamurupara. This was a tale about a couple who got married and lived for years without having any children. They were so sad and would always wish they would have a child. Early one morning they went out of their house and saw a weird old man with an infant wrapped in pigskin. The old man gave them the baby and told them that the baby was a special gift for them and that his name was Induamurupara. The baby grew up and had only one long strand of hair and was totally bald headed.

Induamurupara was hardworking and did all the chores with unbelievable strength but he ate a lot and seemed to leave no food left uneaten in the house. His over eating made his parents overlook how hardworking he was and so decided to get rid of him. They threw him into the fast-flowing river but he didn't drown. They poisoned food and fed it to him but it did nothing to him. They mumu'd him with the kaukaus but he came out alive and well. After all the attempts, Induamurupara came to realise that their love for him had worn off. Before they all went to sleep, he told his parents that if they didn't want him anymore, they only had to pull the lone strand of hair when he was asleep. While he was sleeping his father pulled the hair off his head and when he did so, he felt Induamurupara breathe his last. Oh, this story made us all sad and hate Induamurupara's parents.

I grew up listening to stories from ancient tales to tales of the realms in the forest lands. I remember stories told of our ancestors who were so tall, the last one used to carry people across the Loluai river back in the day.

There were also neighbouring villages where the inhabitants died out to the last one, where one of my father's uncles had to go and bury the last person because there was no one else to bury her. Stories of the smoke of death that the pohurai lit in the middle of the village when the villagers were sleeping was believed to be the witchcraft that caused all villagers to die out.

Another tale recounted the legend of the 'arakamo,' a spectral fire that soared through the night, drawn by the demise of a beloved soul to seek out the perpetrator of the death. Such stories filled us with dread, forbidding us from venturing out after dark. It was believed that if a flame flickered atop a dwelling, it signified that the abode harboured the individual responsible for a recent passing.

My grandmother was the custodian of our cultural heritage, imparting to me a wealth of beliefs, legends, and stories that had been passed down through generations. She spoke of the profound impact of curses uttered in the wake of betrayal, particularly if a loved one fell victim to the 'pohurai' poison. She recounted how the guilty party, driven to madness by the power of spoken curses, would rise at dawn to prepare bananas or kaukaus over the fire, pack them in his 'pukai', and journey to the burial grounds. There, amidst the graves, he would consume his meal alongside the remains of the one whose life he had extinguished.

Nowadays, I find myself pondering the veracity of these tales. As a child, they instilled in me an intense fear. I learned to dispose of my leftovers in the flames, to gather the remnants of sugarcane after chewing, and to guard my possessions vigilantly against the 'pohurai'. I was instructed to be mindful of where I placed my water container and to conceal salt and sugar, for these were the substances most coveted by the 'pohurai'. These practices, ingrained in me from a young age, remain with me; even now, I ensure that no food or water is left unattended in the presence of others. Such caution is a legacy of my upbringing, a testament to the enduring power of our traditions.

I've heard tales of ancient funeral rites practiced by our ancestors. They would fell banana trees and fashion the stems into towering structures. These towers were then adorned with an abundance of greenery, taro, bananas, and coconuts, creating a verdant tribute to the deceased, who was laid to rest at the pinnacle. As the pyre was set ablaze, the air filled with the sounds of lamentation and farewell hymns, guiding the departed on their journey to the afterlife. It was said that the fire's intensity was fuelled by the natural oils and fluids of the human body, a detail vividly recounted by my mamo.

From the way she told me her ancestral stories, I gathered that our ancestors believed that their loved ones who have passed on looked out for them and protected them.

When I was a young person, we always got scared to enter my father's uncle's house, as it was believed that the great warrior chief, who was known as *Kaharai*, his spirit could still be seen hovering around the dark corners. We used to get so petrified when we entered the house.

Even though Christianity had already over taken the livelihoods of my people, they would always try to make sense of the difficult encounters through their ancestral beliefs. It is something that happens in all indigenous cultures.

Some of the scariest times of my childhood was when someone had passed on. The old people back then, did not cry and weep like we do now. They sang ancestral songs that told stories and through these songs they praised the loved one who has passed on, telling them that that they would go thereafter and meet a loved one who was already there. And listening to these lamentations as a child, trying my best to sleep was truly frightening.

I was around 7 to 8 years old, when I experienced spirit-controlled realms in our forest lands. It was the day, I decided to pick the mareua seeds and edible leaves with my mamo. In Tok-Pisin, the name of mareau tree is known as the Tulip tree. The mareua trees are slim with long thin trunks and are left to grow in the forest lands so that their seasonal yields can be enjoyably consumed by the people who are from that certain land or who are the landowners.

On that Friday, mamo and I set out early to the forest lands of the Wukomai ranges, where from Oria village, you can see that Mountain Wukomai is still much higher than the elevated forest lands, that makes the fertile Orian valley. We collected the edible leaves of the mareua plus the edible yellow seeds and packed them in the bags we had brought with us. We had so much fun, imitating and miming various funny characters of known people and conversing in the different dialects of Wisai area and then got carried away, conversing in the Oremai/Sulekunu dialect. For example, in the Oria language, 'You go back' is '*Lo unololora*' but in the Oremai dialect it would be '*Lo mamulolora*' and the voice tempo is lifted up at the end. The Oria dialect, the voice tempo is dropped at the end.

We continued to speak in the Oremai dialect as we picked the *Mareua* leaves and seeds. After we had collected enough to share amongst our extended families, we decided to go on home and through the trees we could see that the sun was above us, confirming that it was around 11 or 12 o'clock. We walked around the forest floor that mamo was familiar with and kept on looking for the path that we would take to return to the village. We walked and walked but kept on ending up where we had started from.

My skinny legs were tired and I kept telling my mamo that I was hungry. "Lo, nene wumoisi" (Hey, we are lost) mamo finally confessed to me, when she realised that she had actually taken me around in circles and the sun which was overhead, when we had started tracking home was below the tree lines. Then she started yelling in the Oria dialect, confirming that she was the daughter of *Kaharai*, the warrior chief and whoever was enticing and confusing her, making her go in circles, with her grandchild, must release us immediately.

We walked on and as she turned the overgrown shrubs on her right, she saw the track leading downwards through the closely clustered numerous ancient trees. We walked on down and then came to Mosina's garden lands and then we kept on walking. As the fireflies came out and about, we were at Wuloli creek. We arrived home in the night and all our extended families came together and listened to mamo's recount of what had happened to us that day.

"Oremai, nono nohu oko oko lohehu, musinkehe mala wuotomasiu, ia nonomata emu ihiko musiakue avivinotoposi," mamo related as she shared our day's gathering of prized mareua leaves and seeds. (*We were conversing in the Oremai dialect and the forest dwellers confused my mind and I took my grandchild, going around in circles until the sun went down.*)

From 1974 to 1976, my father used to buy dry cocoa beans for Buin Society. People, as far and wide from all over Konnou, including the villages in the mountains and lowlands of the Wisai area, which consists of my village Oria, brought their dry cocoa beans to father. He purchased them and stored them in a shed he built. From there, he chartered BougAir (Bougainville Airlines), planes that were owned and operated in Bougainville, to transport the bags of dry cocoa beans to Buin town. When father got on BougAir at around 8am, I would go with him to Buin town and wait for him outside the office, playing stones, with the other staff children, while he dealt with the bags of cocoa beans.

The Buin Society office was right next to the Buin airstrip, so when he finished at around 12pm, we would take a ride in the Buin Society vehicle and go to Buin town. We would eat at Lai Ken & Sons and my favourite was the golden circle pineapple, where I would eat all the chunks and drink the juice, even licking the inside of the tin.

Then after lunch, we did some shopping and then we were brought back to the airstrip to wait for the 3pm flight of the Cessna plane. We'd get on the plane and arrive in Oria around 3:45pm. I can remember all the goodies I brought home to share with my brother and cousins. In those days, all the goodies came from Australia and New Zealand.

One very vivid memory that stands out to me, was cleaning the Kiln pipe for father's cocoa dryer. The Kiln pipe was quite long, between 10 to 20 metres and was where the firewood was thrown into and lit so the cacao beans on the steel wire netting, some metres above the pipe would get smoked and dry.

Since the pipe was small, adults would not fit into it to sweep out the ashes, it and sweep out the ashes, after the cacao beans have been dried and sold. So, I was always getting into the pipe, instructed by my father to sweep out the ashes. Father would use a long pole like rake to pull out all the charcoal and ashes. Then I would crawl through the pipe all the way to the very end, to where the chimney was. In total darkness, in a very narrow space, I would twist my skinny body around and face the light at the front of the pipe, where I had crawled from. Then with the light flat board, I would push all the ashes out, until I reached the end of the pipe, where father would wait and laugh because I would be covered in ashes. I was like a little chimney sweeper but instead of going down and up, I went across the Kiln pipe.

Since the Oria airstrip was built around 1971, the people of Oria and Paghui, plus the surrounding villages, carried quite a large tractor from Buin town, transported to Turutai over rough terrains across the mountain Sansaro, crossing the fast-flowing Aibia River and deep Pirasi river all the way to Oria airstrip. As mentioned earlier, this was the grass cutting tractor, for the Oria airstip and Mosina was in charge and continuously mowed the airstrip and made sure the airplanes landed safely.

The BougAir and Cessna pilots were mainly Australians and New Zealanders. If they landed at Oria airport and terrible weather persisted, they would overnight at our humble abode. It was not long until my father built the first fully permanent house.

In around 1976 to 1977, my father transported all permanent building materials solely through charters on BougAir to Oria and built the first permanent house, apart from the DPI houses. All timbers were treated against termites, the living room chairs and coffee table were exported from Australia through Barclay Brothers furniture and from the house posts to the last item, the house was solely of western materials.

The house still stands today, as I write these words.

My father also was the HEO, at the Kutalehu Aidpost, where he cared for the Oria, Paghui and other surrounding villagers. He gave medication, injections, and dressings that included stitching fresh cuts and advising extended medical treatment at Buin or Arawa hospitals.

We even had people coming to our house in the early hours of the mornings when they needed medical help. I remember a story, of one of my father's clans men who came calling for father in the early hours of the morning. When father, went out to see him, his thigh was slashed clean, with a neat long cut. Father asked him what had happened, and he told my father that he had an encounter with a wild boar and the tusk of the boar did that. No, my father told him. If it was a wild boar, the flesh would be all smashed up, your cut is sliced through with the sharp edge of a blade. "You are right my clansman", the old man told my father. "It was done by a levolevo".

The levolevo is a unique tool, reminiscent of an axe, characterised by itsits slender, elongated axe head. This axe head is carefully crafted and scorched to seamlessly integrate with a svelte, sturdy shaft made of lightweight yet durable wood. The design emphasises a balance between form and function, ensuring the levolevo is both aesthetically pleasing and practical for use.

This levolevo can double as a walking stick, with the axe head serving as a handgrip, its sharp edge protruding prominently. Moreover, the levolevo can be wielded as a protection weapon, allowing its owner to swiftly turn it around and swing the axe head at a target with precision. Historically, the levolevo was a traditional weapon, where obsidian rock was used as the axe head, and warriors would employ it to decapitate their enemies.

Growing up in Oria, I had the opportunity to observe the levolevo first-hand. My father's uncle, kako Billie, would use it as his trusty walking stick. Blind and reliant on others, kako Billie would grasp the axe head in his right hand, while I, as a young girl, would hold the opposite end of the levolevo, guiding him to his desired destinations. Although the axe head was no longer razor-sharp, I realised that it still possessed sufficient potency to protect kako in the event of an attack, should he swing it around with force.

I remember a sad tragedy that happened when I was around 6 or 7 years old. My aunties Namina and Pinaua, opened the large window at our house. Now this window was the largest and there was a waist high tomba that was built across the length of the window. There was a piece of heavy one metre wood that the grownups used to push out the window and then placed the end into a slot. One of my aunties had opened the window as early as around 3:30am, because they were looking out for the men, all the abled men in Oria had gone to look for a man who was cutting down trees in a virgin forest to make a new garden.

This man's name was Elijah and he was my father's friend. I used to see them conversing at the Buin Society warehouse and he would visit our home regularly to talk with my father. Elijah was from the Kongara mountains and he was at Rumba Central School when my father was there. He left his homeland on the border of central and south Bougainville to marry one of my father's relations.

Elijah had not returned for a day or two and all the men had gone to look for him. When I woke to the sound of my aunties talking with my mother, I went over to them and heard the news that Elijah has been found but it was a tragedy. A tree had fallen on him, when he chopped it down. I was terrified as a young child and sat amidst my aunties at the large window looking out onto the path in the darkness where the people who had gone to retrieve the body would walk to the main village.

Before we saw the people, we heard lamentations that echoed through the air from the other side of Pauhu River. Then what stayed with me throughout the years was the men's panting deep voices as they carried the body on a bush stretcher, covered in leaves. We heard the mourning, from men and women who escorted the carriers as they went past our house. I was so frightened and sad at the same time, that a friend of my father's had lost his life in a terrible way, leaving his wife and two children.

I vaguely remember that when I was 6 or 8, I was told to carry a bunch of fresh flowers and was the flower girl at my uncle Ue's wedding to aunty Aretai in our SDA village church. The bride price ceremony took place after the church wedding and I remember a very large long tomba tava that held a lot of store items and garden produce, was about to collapse because of the weight and my relatives were shouting, as they supported the tomba tava with wood and timber.

Aunty Aretai's father, a very close relation of mamo, distributed the bride price, when it was placed in his hands. He distributed it to all of Aretai's relatives and even gave some back to mamo, and the last I saw in his hand was a 20 Kina note.

The other wedding was for aunty Kutamari, who was my step grandfather's niece. She was looked after by mamo and nono since she was a young girl of around 3 or 4 years old. When she grew into a young woman, she returned to her people in the mountains of Wisai.

So when she was getting married, word was sent down to mamo and nono to go to Kokousi and collect her bride price. The family got prepared and with our closest relatives, we carried store goods and walked up the valley terrain to Koukousi. We arrived and were taken to Misa's house, nono's people who were going to receive the bride price with him.

The adults went to prepare Kutamari, and I remember the first time I saw a pig being slaughtered, as I was brought up an Adventist, I had not witnessed anything of that sort. It was scary, as the pig squealed with pain and I couldn't watch any longer so I went to play with the other kids while we waited.

We gathered on the mouroru; Kutamari's relatives on one side and the groom's relatives on the other side. The store goods and garden vegetables from our side went to the groom's people and the one's from the groom's side came to us. Then we watched as Kutamari carried the largest Ahoto, the first I had seen and she walked along the mouroru and then she climbed the steps up to her new husband's house, as we clapped and congratulated them. The old people held a shouting match and jumped here and there with their levolevos but in the end everything quietened down and a feast was laid out for everyone.

The ones who were Adventists were shown a special mumu in Misa's hauskuk. We went ahead, opened the mumu and the food parcels were chicken and taro, creamed with coconut milk. It was so delightful. I can still remember the taros tasted stickily delicious.

New Year's celebrations were the most eagerly anticipated and exhilarating events in Oria, filling the air with an infectious sense of joy and excitement. As Adventist Christians, Christmas was not celebrated but the New Year was the highlight. People were thankful that God had taken care of them throughout the year and that if they had lost loved ones, it was meant to be. So New Year was celebrated to welcome the new year and to set good vibes and happiness for the months to come.

It was a wonderful celebration that I have no idea where people in my village got it from but I believe they invented it. We would start hitting drums and tins walking along the road and tracks throughout all the hamlets in our district. We typically kicked off our New Year's Eve celebrations around 7pm, revelling in the festive atmosphere until the clock struck midnight, marking the dawn of a brand-new year. The cacophony of noise was not only tolerated but actively encouraged, as even the older folks joined in with their own unique brand of revelry.

My father, never one to shy away from making a racket, would fire up his chainsaw at the stroke of midnight, creating an ear-splitting din that echoed through the night air. Meanwhile, Mosina would enthusiastically bang away at a corrugated iron sheet with a large stick, adding to the symphony of sound. Other grown men would chime in with their own contributions, creating a joyous pandemonium that filled the streets.

Later on, when my father acquired his vehicles, he'd take it up a notch, blaring the horn repeatedly until the clock struck 12, much to the delight of everyone around. Hahaha, those were truly unforgettable nights!

Apart from the discordance and revelry, there was also a more melodious side to our New Year's Eve celebrations. Christian groups would go from door to door, spreading joy and cheer through song, and in return, they would be showered with generous donations of cash or kind.

We would take off in the night and walk in darkness, sometimes with a flash light or flames from dried coconut leaves. Then on January the first, there would be partying and feasting, mostly a cow and a lot of chickens were slaughtered and shared amongst the community. Each family or extended families would cook food and come together at the common mouroru and eat, while enjoying a drama or skit put on by family members or singing gospel songs.

The main food in my village back then when I was growing up, was kaukau, bananas, yams, cassava, taros and others plus a variety of green vegetables. There were/are (still is, I believe) a variety of kaukaus that have special names in our language or named after whoever brought it to our village. I remember, my mother named a variety of peanuts 'marlene peanut' because I brought that variety from Rabaul to Oria.

There are also a variety of bananas, variety of yams and there is one very rare and delicious yam my mother used to grow (still grows). In our language we call it porutoro. This yam has a white texture and grew into the ground like large fingers moving in all direction. Yam is creamed with coconut milk and flavoured with herbs like wuhuva.

Our food was always mixed with a variety of green vegetables, whether it be choko or pumpkin tips, mareua, maraham, and cabbages that were in season. Mother used to scatter the seeds of the chinese cabbage and it grew everywhere in her gardens. There was always abundant food sources that spread out into the forest lands as well, wild edible greens, wild yams and wild fruits.

Special food was cooked on Fridays because of the Sabbath which started at 6pm. On Fridays we would make masimasi, kava and scrapped tapiok, which we infused with mashed banana and coconut milk and put it in the mumu.

We ate apilli on most mornings and went off into our gardens, where lunch was taken care of in various ways. Whether we cooked green bananas over open fires or steamed some root vegetables, greens or mushrooms in bamboo tubes. I loved the mushrooms that we loutoi in the open fires.

Dinner was always the main meal in our home, where we ate different varieties of garden and store food plus a source of protein whether it be fish or chicken.

My father and his brother, Ue, were skilled fishermen who plied their trade on the inland rivers. Their frequent fishing expeditions, which took place two to three times a week, would yield an abundance of fresh fish. As a result, our house would often overflow with their bounty, which my mother would carefully smoke over an open fire and store on the tava, filling our home with the savoury aroma of freshly preserved fish.

In addition to the bounty from the rivers, my father was also an avid hunter, who owned shotguns and would venture out to hunt wild birds such as the hornbill, pigeons, and other edible species. Once he returned with his catch, our mother would skillfully smoke the birds, and we would look forward to enjoying them in a traditional mumu feast every Friday. Our house was truly a haven of culinary delights, with a diverse range of dishes always available.

One of my absolute favourite dishes was the breadfruit seed, which was carefully collected during its seasonal peak and then smoked to perfection over the tava for weeks, even months, to bring out its rich flavour. When it was finally ready, it would be lovingly creamed with coconut milk and served alongside kaukau or taros, creating a truly delectable gastronomic experience. My mamo, was the master chef behind this dish, and she would cook it to my heart's content, just the way I loved eating it.

As a child, I would often venture into the cacao plantations and forest lands along the Wuloli creek with my cousins, on a mission to forage for galip nuts. When the galip trees were in season, we'd embark on a treasure hunt, clearing the grasses and shrubs beneath the trees to uncover the prized nuts. Once we'd gathered a sufficient amount, we'd crack them open using stones, revelling in the crunchy white insides. The perfect tools for the job were the pingpings - long, smooth stones that had been passed down through generations.

To crack the nuts, we'd hold the pingping firmly in our right hand, while securing the galip nut in our left hand on another stone. With a swift motion, we'd bring the pingping down to crack the nut, carefully extracting the delicious contents. We'd either devour the galip nuts on the spot or collect them for mother to transform into masimasi.

I was always fascinated by the pingping stones, which stood out among the rougher stones that were more common. One day, I asked mamo why the pingping was so unique. With a knowing glint in her eye, she told me, "Oh, the pingping is dropped on the earth through lightning and thunderstorms." I believed her wholeheartedly back then, but now I realise that she was passing down a story that had been orated through generations, a tale that had been shared with her by her own elders.

Our supply of smoked and dried galips, as well as dried sago, would arrive courtesy of our grandfather, kako Kauva, who would travel all the way from Tugiogu to bring us these exotic indigenous delicacies in Oria. He would carefully package the galips in three-meter-long bamboo tubes, drying them to perfection on the tava before embarking on the long journey to deliver them to us. Similarly, the sago would be wrapped in sago palms and rolled into one-meter-long oblongs, which he would consistently deliver to our doorstep, bringing a taste of our cultural heritage to our table.

When we visited our beloved Teite in Tugiogu, she would greet us with a traditional gesture of affection, kissing us from our toes all the way up to our cheeks. This was a cherished custom from her roots in Daulo district, Nonambaro village, in the Eastern Highlands Province.

Teite was also an avid poultry keeper, with a thriving flock of chickens that she raised in a sturdy enclosure built with long, tough sticks. The hens would even lay eggs in the baskets and boxes she strategically placed under her stilted house. And just a stone's throw away from her home, a bounty of galip trees stood tall, providing us with a daily harvest of fresh galips, which we would collect every morning during our visit.

Taraha, the serene creek near my grandparents' house, was a treasured spot where we would bathe and fetch drinking water from the crystal-clear spring that bubbled from the cliff walls. The creek's banks were lined with an endless array of sago palms, and even on the hottest days, the water remained refreshingly cold. My aunt Lucia and I would often venture to a specific part of Taraha, where a sago palm had been chopped down, and search for grubs in the soft, fibrous trunk. We'd collect the grubs and take them back to mother, who would roast them over the fire and savour them as a delicacy. On Fridays, I'd accompany my teite to Piano Catholic Station, where we'd sell chicken eggs or fresh vegetables from her garden, enjoying the lively atmosphere and warm interactions with the local community.

School days

'Learning opens the window to the world'

My mother Margaret started teaching me at home when I turned five years old. My cousins came to our home school too, but they mostly didn't understand what mother tried to get across to our village brains. After two years of home schooling, I was then enrolled at Hairu Adventist School to do grade one in 1978.

My first teacher was Mr. Timothy Ambi from Paghui village, our relations in the next village up an amazing hill. I can still remember those school days from grades one to two, as rowdy and unorganised classroom learning. The classrooms were overcrowded with us village troupers, harnessed to settle in a secured hot thriving area to learn ah, eh ih oh uh and the 1 2 3 4 5, that we sang with untrained loud ear racking tunes.

We were rowdy indeed, as we shouted at each other and instead of building with blocks, we threw them at each other as well. We were real twits. It was really awful, when I look back now. But the really good thing was everyone always survived the first two years of school there at Hairu, so I am truly glad I did.

It is also quite vivid that I encountered bullying by grown grade 5 – 6 females, when I was in grades 1 and 2. There was one particular bully, who used to continuously scare me with fat black worm like critters that lived in the soil between the crotons that we weeded. I would shudder and start to cry and then she would laugh, until one day, a certain female, who was from Pauluaku village, told her fiercely to lay off and stop what she was doing to me.

The older females at the school were notorious for their fierce behaviour. They would often torment certain students who had travelled from afar to attend the school, pushing them to the brink of insanity. I vividly remember one incident where they orchestrated a fight between two female students who were boarders from outside Oria and Paghui. On other occasions, these older females would lead us younger students in dangerous and mischievous games. One such game involved capturing a young boy from grade 5, who was known for his mischievous ways, and holding him by his legs and arms. They would then swing him around as if he was in a hammock, before releasing him abruptly onto the lawn. The poor boy would get up, furious and disoriented, and chase after us. We had to be quick to escape his wrath. If he managed to catch one of the little girls, the older girls from grades 5 and 6 would gang up on him, holding him down and subjecting him to the same treatment. This chaotic game would continue until the lone boy would finally give up and flee home, exhausted and humiliated.

When I entered grade 3, I found that the classroom environment was more structured and conducive to learning, and my fellow students and I were more focused and enthusiastic about acquiring knowledge. Our grade 3 teacher, the exceptional Mrs. Lily Tovilu, played a significant role in fostering this positive atmosphere. Under her guidance, I began to excel in school, and my parents were overjoyed by my progress. I developed a deep passion for reading, devouring books from the Raka, Ranu, Tabu, and Noka series, as well as stories about Mr. White's teaching adventures and camping trips. The Melanesian and Pacific Series were particularly captivating, and they sparked a love for reading that would stay with me for years to come.

In grade 3, I also discovered the joy of writing stories and recognised the importance of reading in understanding the world around me. I realised that most of the knowledge I gained was through self-directed reading, and I became hooked, spending hours poring over books from my father's collection, who was an avid reader himself. As I delved deeper into the world of reading, I became more introverted, but this newfound love also allowed me to gain a deeper understanding of the world and its complexities.

When I entered grade 4, my cousins from Oria got enrolled to attend Hairu school, where they all started in grade 1. Every morning, we'd walk to school together, a lively bunch of village kids. As we arrived, the boys would scatter to join their friends, while the girls would stick with me. We were a carefree and lively group, each with our own unique personalities. My cousin Katherine, affectionately known as Kaida, was particularly strong-willed and assertive, often taking charge and bossing us around - and we'd listen to her without hesitation. Not only did she lead us, but she also protected us fiercely, never hesitating to stand up to anyone who dared to mess with her siblings. This cherished memory remains vivid in my mind, and I'm certain Kaida hasn't forgotten it either.

There was this one time, after the work parade, I headed to our grade four classroom to retrieve my homework book, accompanied by my cousins Kaida, Sevina, Kiatui, and Yangula. Suddenly, our class monitor, Siughu, appeared and ordered my cousins to leave the classroom, citing that it wasn't their designated area. Everyone quickly exited, except for Katherine, who stood her ground and assertively told Siughu that she had every right to wait for me inside, as we were cousins and would be walking home together. Siughu insisted that she wait outside, but Katherine refused to back down. The situation escalated when Siughu threatened to hit her, prompting Katherine to dash around the rows of desks and flee out to the lawn. I thought the confrontation had ended, but Katherine let out a loud scream, hurling a stinging insult at Siughu, telling him to 'go smoke his mother's brus pipe.' Siughu was deeply offended and gave chase, pursuing Katherine around the school grounds. The two of them clashed, with Siughu eventually tackling her to the ground. Despite being a bigger and stronger boy, Katherine refused to yield. Siughu struck her with a stick, and they rolled around on the grass until a group of older boys from Oria intervened, throwing Siughu off and chasing him into the nearby bushes.

I still vividly recall the aftermath of that brutal fight - Katherine's face and arms were badly bruised, her clothes were torn, and she looked like she was on the verge of collapse. I was terrified, my heart racing with fear. Yangula, Sevina, Kiatui, and I were overcome with emotion, sobbing uncontrollably as we guided Katherine to the Pauhu river, where she bathed her wounds. We then escorted her home, still shaken by the intensity of the altercation.

During our carefree days, we'd often spend hours swimming in the Pauhu river, which served as the lifeblood of Oria, providing a convenient spot for the villagers to bathe, wash their cooking utensils, and do their laundry. I vividly recall the times we'd stumble upon a gentleman's underwear caught between the stones, which we'd then dry in the sun. Next, we'd search for a stick with a Y-shaped top, and use it to create a makeshift contraption. We'd stretch the underwear over the stick, securing both ends to the Y-shaped edges, and then drop a large pebble or stone into the fabric. The absurdity of it all would leave us in stitches, and we'd laugh until the sun dipped below the horizon. As the day drew to a close, our mothers would call out to us, their yodelling voices echoing through the valley, signalling it was time to head back home.

I fondly recall the times when my cousins and I would venture into the bushes, where we'd build thatched huts, complete with a fire pit for cooking. We'd roast tomea bananas over the open flames, savouring the sweet, caramelized flavour. The areas where we built our huts would often double as our 'toy gardens,' a term my mother affectionately used to describe these miniature plots. We'd cultivate these gardens along the Oria airstrip, growing a variety of crops, including grape tomatoes, aibikas, corn, kaukau, tomea bananas, and an assortment of leafy greens like hurinampo and rekai. These traditional greens, passed down from my matrilineal grandmother's homeland, were incredibly flavoursome, and we developed a strong fondness for them. The memories of those carefree days, spent playing and gardening in the bush, remain vivid in my mind.

I am a born gardener, and the allure of the soil and lush greenery has a profound effect on me, no matter where I roam in Papua New Guinea. This innate passion is evident in the pot plants that I lovingly tend to, a testament to my enduring connection with the natural world.

One of my closest friends from the village, Stella Keka, was also a relative of mine. We started attending Hairu school together, and before long, we became inseparable, walking to and from school as a duo. Our mischievous streak soon emerged, and we'd often sneak around the Pisokokui hamlet gulley, pilfering juicy mangoes from the Pusua's mango tree. Little did we know that the very same mango tree would one day become a part of Stella's life, as she would eventually marry Joseph Pusua. The irony of it all still brings a smile to my face - haha!

Stella, Otu, Yangula, and I once huddled behind a shed after school, seeking refuge from the rain, and watched the boys play soccer in the downpour. We munched on a long packet of chocolate cream biscuits, giggling over silly things. Then, Stella started teasing a boy named Pauku, who was from Paghui village, calling out to him and telling him that his mother had sent a biscuit for him. When Pauku turned our way, Stella pretended to look the other way. Otu, my aunt, my father's first cousin, and Billy's daughter (may her soul rest in peace), kept warning Stella to stop, as the boys might come and beat us up. Stella would refrain for a while, but due to the pouring rain and the long wait for it to stop, she'd start again. I'm sure she was doing it out of boredom. She called out to Pauku to come and get his biscuit. Pauku ran over to us, demanding that Stella hand over the biscuit, but she told him to get lost. Pauku retaliated by whacking her across her arm. Stella yelled some uncivilized obscenities at Pauku, and we all took off, running for our lives in the rain, down the slippery hill to our village Oria. I sprinted away like a young ostrich with long, wobbly skinny legs. Otu was hot on my heels, and Yangula and Stella brought up the rear. Otu and I reached the Pauhu river, but didn't see Stella, except for Yangula, who was stumbling towards us. We ran back and, on the next drop, saw Stella lying in the choko garden that belonged to Singkasi, beaten by Pauku. A wild taro had been placed on top of her, and Pauku had left her there. We helped her up and took her down to the river Pauhu, where she washed her grimy body. Then, we all swam in the river and walked home, laughing and yelling with uncivilised abandon.

As I mentioned earlier, Oria was inaccessible by road, with the Buin Highway ending at Turutai, the village situated at the foot of Mount

Sansaro, and the Arawa Highway ending at Lolilu, on the banks of the Loluai River. To reach Arawa, we would embark on a two-hour walk down to Lolilu, where our uncle Kia would pick us up and transport us to our destination. However, we were fortunate to have a more time-efficient option - the busy air transport service, which operated from the Oria airstrip conveniently located right next to our house.

Before the highway even reached our village, when Hornibrooks and Bismarck were just starting to occupy the Lolilu banks with their earthmoving equipment, my father bought a Toyota vehicle - one of those open-back models, I'm not sure of the exact model.

At that time, the highway had not yet reached Oria village, but some of the road machinery, including bulldozers, had already made their way through the thick forests. The surveyors were busy monitoring which areas were suitable for the highway, as the terrain from Lolilu to the Oria valley presented a challenge, with lowlands, swamps, and blocked streams that flowed into the forest lands.

However, there was an alternative route that provided quicker access; the Ruaki road, named after a local landowner and distant relative of my father from the Wisai area. Ruaki had taken the initiative to clear a path through the trees, allowing for faster access to Kulula, a Catholic mission station.

Before the highway reached Oria, my father would drive the Toyota to Kovolai, a cacao plantation owned by Pusua, a relative of my father. Located adjacent to the Ruaki road and opposite the Lulivai river, the plantation served as a convenient stopping point. During that time, the mighty Loluai river lacked a bridge, forcing all vehicles to ford the currents, which had been partially cleared of large stones by Bismarck's earthmovers, making the crossing even more perilous.

Our journey began with a two-and-a-half-hour walk to Kovolai, after which we climbed aboard the Toyota. My father drove us down the Ruaki road; I recall there might have been a fee for using this private thoroughfare, though I'm not entirely certain. The drive to Arawa town was lengthy, and upon our return, he parked the vehicle at Kovolai, marking the start of our extended trek to Oria village.

In time, the path to Oria was cleared by a bulldozer, allowing my father to drive up to the residence of nono Kaleva (may his beautiful soul rest in peace), located beside Hairu Primary School. Despite this progress, a drivable road to Oria village remained non-existent. We usually left the vehicle at nono Kaleva's and embarked on another half-hour walk, navigating the meandering trail down to the river Pauhu, followed by the ascent into the Oria valley, ending in our arrival at the village.

When the bulldozer was working at a slow progress, the path or track up to the village was cleared with grass knives and dug up with spades and father drove his vehicle right to the foot of our house.

Until FINALLY, the road was properly bulldozed after a year or so.

That just showed how impatient Oria people are. They are hands on people, who do not prefer sitting around and waiting for things to happen.

When I was in 4th grade in 1981, a terrible event occurred that would leave an indelible mark on my life. The next day, when I went to school, kids looked at me weirdly and whispered about the situation. I stood at the back of the classroom, overcome with emotion, and cried.

What had happened was that my father had driven our Toyota to Arawa, accompanied by my mamo, my younger brother, and some other relatives. On their return journey from Arawa, the weather was calm, but when they arrived at Lolilu, where Hornibrooks was still constructing the bridge, my father realised that the Loluai River was flooding. He quickly shifted the vehicle into four-wheel drive and started crossing the river at the usual spot. However, as he reached the middle of the river, where the current was strongest, the engine died.

My father tried to restart the engine, but it wouldn't spark back to life. A message was sent to one of the earthmoving machines to help tow the vehicle, but in a split second, the floodwaters surged, lifting the Toyota off where it was. Everyone on board began struggling and swimming to the riverbank, fighting against the powerful currents. My father managed to grab my brother and battle his way to the river bank, while my grandmother was helped and carried to safety by a stranger she didn't recognise. She would later recount how the man was tall and strong, carrying her across the flooded river with ease, making her feel safe. We always believed that an angel had saved her.

By the time the earthmovers arrived, it was too late. My father's first-ever Toyota, which he had driven to the village through a man-made track, had been swept away by the Loluai flood, its body grinding against the rocks. Two days after the floodwaters had receded, the vehicle was found smashed and stuck between two large rocks. Unfortunately, thieves had already stripped it of its parts, leaving it a hollow shell, impossible to tow.

Mr. Boaz Ambi, was our grade 6 teacher and he was a very good one. He was truly committed and taught us a variety of subjects and introduced what he called morning talk, where we were scheduled each morning after devotion before class started to stand in front of the class and present an interesting talk. I loved this part of the morning, I truly did. I sat up at night preparing my morning talk and practiced speaking properly, so I would sound like an intelligent fluent English speaker. But truthfully, our tongues were so heavy with our mother tongue dialects, that speaking English was quite a task, but writing stories was all right. It was the speaking and re-telling it, that was indeed difficult.

Mr. Ambi wouldn't let anyone speak in Pidgin. We had some really good laughs, when classmates stood on one foot, scratched their heads vigorously and stuttered weird English vocabulary. I can still remember a story I shared during morning talk. This story was told to me by aunty Aretai, my uncle Ue's wife. The story was about a little girl named Lily, who went down to the spring quite late to fill her container with water and a monstrous frog came out of the bog and swallowed her. Then the frog was butchered by the villagers and Lily jumped out of its watery stomach unharmed. It was a stupid little children's story, but Mr. Ambi was really impressed with the way I told it and congratulated me. I was truly proud of myself, as I realised that the many nights that I practiced speaking English and re-telling stories I've heard from my family, had finally paid off, with my teacher's congratulatory message.

As a Unit leader in one of our Pathfinder groups, I recall a particularly memorable incident. During one of our Pathfinder activities, we were competing against other units in various scouting and girl guide-type events. My team and I were building a makeshift stretcher to race against another unit, and in the chaos of it all, my teammate Evano lifted a bush knife to cut the rope. At the same moment, I bent down, and the sharp end of the knife accidentally slipped into the soft tissue above my left eye. It was through God's grace and protection that the knife did not pierce my eye. However, the wound was bleeding severely, and our team immediately dropped all activities, as we were all terrified by the close call.

I completed grade six in 1983 and passed with good marks. I was then accepted to do grade 7 at Kambubu Adventist High school in East New Britain in 1984.

As my departure for Kambubu drew near, my mamo Kovou, kept reminding me that she would deeply miss me. Indeed, I was very close to my mamo, despite our occasional arguments and scolding; I truly loved that dear old woman (may her beautiful soul rest in peace). My aunt, Parei, Kiatui's mother, also kept reminding me that I would soon be leaving for another province and that I should stop wearing those short shorts, which I had grown accustomed to wearing while scaling the forest lands. She urged me to start dressing more like a lady.

In mid-January, my family bid me a tearful farewell at Aropa airport. I was going to deeply miss my two brothers, and my sister Linda had already been crying for a week beforehand. I hugged my crying mother tightly, while my father smiled at me through his dark sunglasses. My mother's sister, Sharon, accompanied me on the Air Niugini flight, and I was heartbroken to be leaving my family and village, Oria, behind. As a forest roaming village kid, I had never been away from home before.

Upon arrival in Rabaul, my beautiful Aunt Mary (may her soul rest in peace), welcomed me warmly at the airport. She hugged and kissed me on both cheeks, and I instantly took a liking to her. She remains my favourite Aunt on my mother's side to this day. (I was still writing this memoir when she passed away.) Aunt Mary took me to her home, where I met her two children, my cousins Sharon and her little brother Spencer.

Over the weekend, on Sunday, they drove me to Kambubu, and I was struck by the school's isolation. It was far from Rabaul, and I felt lonelier than ever. I was overcome with homesickness when I first arrived at Kambubu, despite having Stella, Betty, and other relatives from Oria and Paghui there as well.

Kambubu was a truly alien environment for me, with its monotonous tapioca menu in the dining hall for recess, lunch, and dinner, and its relentless, seven-day-a-week program schedule.

Students from all around the New Guinea Islands, as well as some from Papua and the New Guinea mainland, converged on Kambubu, making it a melting pot of cultures.

I found it challenging to sleep at night in the old dormitory, with its creaky wooden floorboards. I was terrified of a Mrs. Boots entity, who would patrol the corridors, her boots making ominous tapping sounds that echoed through the night. Stella and I would huddle together every night, listening to that eerie boot tapping, back and forth, along the corridor. In the morning, the thirty or so girls in our dorm would snicker and laugh at us, teasing us about conversing in our mother tongue during the midnight hour. But we didn't care. We were frightened children, plucked from the comforts of our homes in Oria, and thrust into this unfamiliar environment by the forces of education.

As part of my Kambubu experience, I was also assigned to the farm work parade list. Every day, we'd trek up to farms 1, 2, 3, 4, and 5 to tackle physically demanding tasks. I particularly loathed cutting the karapa, a task that seemed to sap my energy. Growing up in the village, my parents had never handed me a dull knife and stood over me, barking orders to weed the karapa or other stubborn grasses. Back in Oria, I was accustomed to weeding soft grass in the peanut fields, taking breaks whenever I pleased.

The farm work parades during my first year at Kambubu were brutal. I fell ill frequently, and the monotonous food in the mess hall only added to my misery.

I was truly amazed by my own resilience as I successfully navigated through grade 7, and not only did I survive, but I also returned the following year for grade 8. On the evening of my return to school, I attended a church worship session and found myself seated next to a tall, slim, and stunning girl. Little did I know that this chance encounter would mark the beginning of a beautiful friendship with my lifelong companion, Paula Malepo, now known as Paula Wiemers.

She currently resides in Germany, where she showcases her unique clothing line and organises her own Pacific catwalk shows to model her exquisite designs.

The year 1985 turned out to be a much brighter one with Paula by my side as my best friend. The tapioca served in the mess hall tasted delightful, the task of weeding karapa no longer felt like an insurmountable challenge, and the new dormitory was free from the haunting sounds of mysterious footsteps echoing in the night.

When I was in grade 8, our English teacher, Mr. Tole, decided to climb a coconut tree near his house one Sunday. As he held onto the keel, it suddenly came off, causing the poor guy to come crashing down to the ground. A helicopter was summoned and promptly airlifted Mr. Tole to the Nonga Base hospital. Sadly, he never returned to Kambubu. It wasn't until around eleven years ago in Lae that I crossed paths with him again. I found him seated in his wheelchair, which he had been confined to since the coconut accident.

Following Mr. Tole's hospitalisation due to the fall, Mrs. Morimai took over the role of teaching us English in grade 8. Her approach to Grammar and Vocabulary made the subjects truly captivating, and the literary works she introduced us to, such as "Island of the Blue Dolphins" and "Swift Arrow," were nothing short of exceptional. The stories transported us to new worlds and left us in awe of their beauty and depth.

My enthusiasm for learning soared during this time, and I found great joy in the company of my friends and fellow students. Paula and I developed a Sunday ritual of cooking rice in our well-used pot, the blackened surface telling tales of countless meals. We would add a generous amount of black sauce to the rice, turning it a deep shade of black as it simmered to perfection. The unconventional dish of black sauced rice became a cherished part of our shared experiences, which we savoured alongside gulps of warm tank water.

During my time in grade 9, my work duties shifted to on-campus responsibilities. One vivid memory that stands out is the incident involving some farm girls returning to school on a tractor after a day's work in farm 5, nestled in the mountains.

Paki, the farm manager, seemed to channel his inner race car driver as he navigated the rugged mountain trail with alarming speed. However, as he approached the final corner leading to the lowlands, a mishap occurred – the tractor's trailer detached from the front part, causing chaos and mayhem. The sudden separation sent the girls tumbling in all directions, resulting in a scene of chaos and injuries. Some suffered broken arms, while others sustained cuts and bruises on various parts of their bodies.

Among the victims was my friend Vivian Vai, whose father was a teacher at Hairu Primary School in my village of Oria. Vivian was particularly unfortunate, bleeding from the mouth despite no visible external cuts or injuries. The confusion surrounding her condition persisted until she was brought to Vunapope Catholic Hospital that night for further assessment and treatment.

Upon examination, the doctors discovered that Vivian had sustained a serious injury to her mouth during the accident. The impact had caused her four upper teeth to shift upwards towards her nose, necessitating their removal and replacement with dentures. It was a challenging and painful ordeal for poor Vivian, but she showed remarkable resilience throughout the entire process.

Kambubu was such a very big area and the sea was truly magnificent without doubt. We would go swimming on Sundays and those who knew how to fish with fishing lines did so, while others ate seaweed with dried coconuts. Paula and I just swam and cooked tapioca over open fires and did our black sauced rice and danced around the fire, breathing in the lovely sea breeze and looking across to New Ireland on the horizon.

I really enjoyed the practical side of Agriculture with our teacher Mr. Jacob Steven. He was such a lovely person, who talked to all the students in a kind tone of voice. We made gardens in measured out appointed plots. I really enjoyed planting the Pak choy cabbages, the corn, peanuts, beans and nurturing the aupa kumus around my garden plot.

Needle craft class was a constant struggle for me, a class where I felt utterly inadequate in the art of threading a needle. The simple act of coaxing the thread through the tiny eye of the needle felt like an insurmountable challenge, leaving me frustrated and disheartened. The scissors, once wielded with precision by others, seemed unwieldy in my hands, and the manual labour of operating the sewing machine felt cumbersome and foreign.

My disdain for needle craft extended to my sartorial preferences as well. I harboured a deep aversion towards homemade blouses, favouring the polished aesthetic of factory-made T-shirts. The mandatory dress code for Sabbath worship dictated my attire, relegating me to don dresses against my personal inclinations. The school uniform, with its structured design and collar, offered a semblance of acceptance, especially as my adolescent frame filled out with a touch of added weight. The transition from the old uniform, devoid of a collar and hanging straight down, accentuated my slender figure, emphasizing my tall, lanky stature as I navigated the complexities of teenagehood.

When I was in Grade 9, Mrs. Ward was my English teacher and I soared in Grammar, as well as Oral Vocabulary. Mrs. Ward, saw the love I had for books and encouraged me to borrow books, she'd showed me from the school library. I hated Math plus those sewing classes were such a drag that I was less excited going to them.

Home Economics classes were okay, because we cooked or did the recipe and then ate them all. I loved it as it was such a change from consuming all the tapioca in the mess. Once, we were peeling vegetables and after everything was washed up, Miss Emily Peter, a practical teacher from PAU, asked me to go and empty the peels in the bucket out to the sea, which was at the back of the Home Economics building. I quickly went and empty the bucket and then, as we were doing the chopping, baking and frying, Mrs. Bondou our Home Economics teacher started yelling at everyone about what happened to her nuts, which were in the bucket. Everyone kept looking at me and Miss Emily had this guilty 'oh no' look on her face. I owned up and Mrs. Bondou told me to go right back to the beach where I had poured out the peels and collected all her nuts back. I got the bucket and went back to the beach and saw the nuts floating everywhere on the water. I collected them, until my uniform was wet. Then put them all in the bucket and took the bucket back to the Home Economics room. Everyone was laughing, especially Miss Emily but I didn't see the humour in it. Actually, I was totally pissed off. I couldn't stand those women and students in there and dispersed as soon as the subject bell went.

I loved playing basketball and joined in the friendly games between the students. I loved seeing the ball sunk through the hole, into the basket, as I threw it with my hands. It was a beautiful sight and was pretty cool.

In 1987, I went back to Kambubu to do my grade 10. It was a fascinating year, as I turned 17 and got my hormones truly tickling with boy meets girl truly in the air. Again, sewing in needlecraft was still a very useless thing for me, as my skinny fingers kept getting stuck in the treadle and the cotton refused to go through the needle hole. Mrs. Bondou's, 'Potoura, you are really rough,' 'Potoura you really have to concentrate,' 'Potoura, please, how did you do your hemming?' Goodness, it never ended, as I was just really useless with the needle and to be truthful, I didn't have the heart to learn, as I realised it was just not my kind of thing.

English classes reached new heights under the guidance of Mr. Brooker. Immersed in captivating Reading and Comprehension exercises, as well as engaging writing tasks, I found myself fully engrossed in the quest to impress Mr. Brooker and excel in our Grade 10 national examinations.

I adored Mr. Brooker's classes, and to add to the allure, he had a fascinating background—he had served in the Australian army and spent time in Vietnam before settling in Arawa and marrying the beautiful Nancy from the outer Islands of Bougainville. My classmate, Marina Siori, and I were positioned right at the forefront of the 10A class, eagerly immersing ourselves in Mr. Brooker's enthralling recounts on the extracts of the 'Planet of the Apes' and the 'Strange Case of Dr. Jekyll Mr. Hyde.'

Upon delving into the pages of the 'Strange Case of Dr. Jekyll Mr. Hyde,' I drew my own conclusions, reflecting on the duality of human nature depicted in the characters. The juxtaposition of good and evil within a single individual resonated deeply with me, serving as a poignant reminder of the complexities of morality in our world.

Once Marina and I did something unusually good, that Mr. Brooker presented us with chocolates the next morning. We were so thrilled, we moved up to cloud number nine and felt very special. The boys in our class kept yapping that Mr. Brooker was a *wantok system face*, because his wife was Bougainvillean, but Marina and I closed our ears and went out the door to enjoy our chocolates.

Our class patron in Grade 10A was Mr. Thompson, and he was wonderfully eccentric. We all adored him. He was a highly effective, hands-on Science and Agriculture teacher who taught us about yeast and its leavening properties. He would then lead us outdoors to measure land and dig up soil, seemingly without a specific purpose other than to examine the soil particles.

To reward our hard work, he would invite us to his home and treat us to delectable Caucasian cuisine, a welcome departure from the bland tapioca served in the mess hall. While Mrs. Thompson led the church choir and was a sociable and talkative woman, Mr. Thompson was an introverted and industrious individual who preferred cultivating watermelons that sprawled across the roofs of sheds, yielding prized fruits.

One memorable weekend, Mr. Thompson treated the Grade 10A class to a camping excursion to Marai, nestled in the direction of Pomio. The trip was filled with joy and excitement, culminating in a Saturday night campfire gathering where we baked a damper and held a delightful mini-concert on the pristine white sands by the sea.

During the festivities, Mr. Thompson regaled us with a whimsical song about a three-legged man, showcasing his creativity by dancing with a boot adorned with the number three, cleverly affixed to a stick tucked inside the traditional laplap he wore. The performance was truly captivating and added a touch of humorousness to the evening.

Mrs. Bondou and the grade 10 girls decided to sew their own graduation dresses, with little jackets which they screen printed the bird of paradise on them. The girls did excellently, while my dress with the jacket looked like something the south westerly wind dug up from 'the other side'. I hated that dress and couldn't wait to take it off on that day. I can still remember that it was the worst dress I have ever worn in front of a thousand people. Hahaha.

Our Grade 10 class of 1987 held a significant place in our hearts, as it coincided with Kambubu's Jubilee year, marking a momentous occasion in the school's history. To commemorate this milestone, we were presented with special certificates, symbolising our graduation during Kambubu's Silver Jubilee year.

Following our graduation from Grade 10, I returned to the idyllic beauty of my beloved Bougainville, specifically to Oria village, where I once again found solace in wandering the familiar bushlands of my childhood, reconnecting with the serene landscapes that had shaped my upbringing.

School Teacher

In 1988, at 18 years of age, I went to Sonoma Adventist college to take up the Primary Teaching Course for two years. It was quite a change from Kambubu, mostly the surrounding area was not so vast, free and open like the area around Kambubu. There were still out of bound areas like all other Adventist schools do. The students at Sonoma College, were mature and were ready to be trained to go out into the field to work. The married students' houses were at the edge of the college grounds and the dormitories were in the middle of the campus, closer to the chapel and classrooms.

Attending College during the first year was okay, but most of the male students were always seriously looking around and I sort of was fed up of young men wanting to talk to me. I actually couldn't believe it all, because I was all bones and wasn't much to look at. I was 18, but not matured enough in that area of serious boyfriend girlfriend issues and mostly sat dumbfounded and didn't know how to converse, when I was asked to meet and try to talk. It was a task I was truly not keen on trying and not long after I was left alone, which suited me just fine.

I had a classmate from high school, Longovina Enoch in the same teaching course at Sonoma. I had female classmates from the Solomon Islands and most of my male classmates were from Eastern Highlands, while one was from the Gulf and William Iga was from Central Province.

To make things brighter from all the other unnecessary bits, Mr. and Mrs. Ward got transferred to Sonoma College to teach in the Education Department. I felt so lucky and enjoyed all the lessons, that were presented by all the Lecturers. We did our weekly practical teaching at Sonoma Demonstration School and I was finally realising the hidden teacher traits in me and working quite hard to do well enough to graduate.

My father Nehemiah called me by phone, close to second term holiday and told me that during that holiday, I had to go home, because my uncle Ue was sick and was not doing very well. I had already heard from my mother that he was unwell and over the Christmas holidays, he had an on and off run of illnesses.

I went home to Bougainville for holidays and walked into the hospital room in Arawa and only saw aunty Aretai sitting on the floor with Marian, when she was about one years old. Aunty Aretai came forward, hugged me and we cried and she told me to sit on uncle Ue's bed and wait, as he was taking a shower. I sat there and waited, as my parents conversed with aunty Aretai. Then the door opened and uncle Ue walked over to us and I had the shock of my life. I sobbed like a crazy young woman.

Truthfully, this was the man, who carried me on his young shoulders and upon his muscular chest. He was my father's only brother and I was the one he was always carrying around when I was a child.

Now his stomach, his abdomen was overly swollen and his eyes were large. All his beautiful thick hair had fallen off and his legs doubled up with the water in his body that has gone frenzy.

I hugged him and cried my heart out in front of all the other patients that were in the room, who in my mind didn't exist, only I was in the room with my uncle Ue. My family all sat around and waited for me as I sobbed and hugged my dear uncle Ue, until the doctor came around to make her rounds as I sniffed quietly and watched.

Even as we drove home to Oria that afternoon, I sat at the back of our Hilux and sobbed thinking of my uncle Ue. All the other passengers that my father picked up at the Tankanupe store to take to Buin were confused at the way I was sobbing sadly and looking out to the shoreline.

When we arrived in Oria and drove into our hamlet Nakomai, I jumped off the vehicle and went straight up to my room and cried myself to sleep. This was the first real heartache I felt, as a young woman. I couldn't believe that my uncle Ue was like that now, and that illness was an enemy that eats away all the beauty in our beings. Uncle Ue nurtured me as a baby and watched me grow, teaching me to kick the ball and even placed me among the boys with his word, so that I could play soccer too. Being sick like that was a terrible blow to me and I was totally heart broken.

I did not want to return to Sonoma College and spent my time at Arawa Hospital with aunty Aretai and uncle Ue. My father Nehemiah had a private talk with his brother Ue and then when I went to the hospital to visit Uncle Ue, he called me over to him, hugged me and told me that I needed to return to college and complete my teacher training. He said that he would still be alive when I returned for Christmas holidays. He put a K100 in my hand and made me promise to return to college.

Saying good bye was so hard, because I knew in my heart that uncle Ue, would be gone when I returned. I cried my heart out and my mother Margaret had to come and console me. Uncle Ue cried too, as I can still see him wiping those tears from his eyes, as he sat on that white hospital bed.

I returned to Sonoma college, after having extra weeks at home in Bougainville. I quickly fell into the college routine and got on with my studies. I finally caught up with all my work and at the end of the year, my GPA looked quite good. I went home for Christmas holidays and as soon as my father stopped the vehicle, I jumped off and ran to the cemetery and sat on uncle Ue's grave and cried my heart out. My cousin Kiatui and others came over and cried with me. My mamo Kovou wept to the graveyard with her walking stick, as she lamented her traditional song of sorrow, heart ache and brokenness. We wept at the graveyard until the dusk came creeping in and then we all went home slowly.

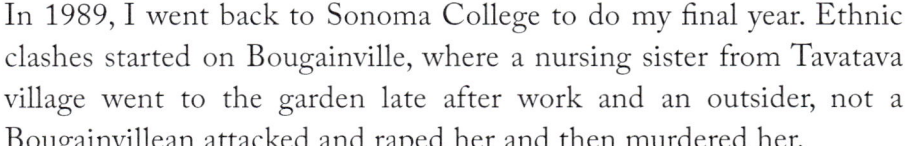

In 1989, I went back to Sonoma College to do my final year. Ethnic clashes started on Bougainville, where a nursing sister from Tavatava village went to the garden late after work and an outsider, not a Bougainvillean attacked and raped her and then murdered her.

Bougainvilleans all retaliated and wanted all outsiders from all over Papua New Guinea and around the world to leave. The redskins, (the name is given to Papua New Guineans due to their skin colouring as being much lighter than that of Bougainvilleans), were suddenly the enemy and they fled Bougainville by planes and ships. Hundreds who were married to Bougainvilleans stayed back and didn't want to leave, as they were protected by their in-laws and felt safe.

When this 'Bougainville versus redskin' clash was on, the Panguna[1] copper mine issue was brewing as well and gradually surfacing. Everything then happened so suddenly, and even I was flabbergasted and confused with what was taking place on beautiful Bougainville.

The talk in college was about Bougainville and the war brewing like crazy, as we heard names of local forces like the militants, rebels and the BRA. The preachers in church preached to say the crisis was one of the signs and wonders of the last days, scaring me as I was not ready for heaven. I was truly worried about my family and my beautiful home. I couldn't wait for the year to end so I could join my family back in my home Bougainville.

For Sonoma college's special six weeks teaching practicum session, our class was scheduled to go to Goroka in Eastern Highlands Province. Cheryl Garimas a Bougainvillean classmate and I, were not on the list to go to Goroka because of the ethnic clashes between the Bougainvilleans and redskins, instead our tickets were booked to go to Barava Central School, in Arawa Bougainville to do our practical teaching there.

When we went to Arawa, I saw that the whole township and everywhere from Panguna, Loloho, Kieta, Toniva and the Aropa airport, were infested with Papua New Guinea soldiers. They were everywhere

---

1 - The Panguna mine is a large copper mine located in Bougainville. It is one of the largest copper reserves in Papua New Guinea and in the world, with an estimated one billion tonnes of ore copper and twelve million ounces of gold. BCL was majority owned by global mining group Rio Tinto, but operations ceased after the armed insurgency known as the "Bougainville Crisis". Significant and widespread environmental damage (which continues to this day,) and the limited financial compensation paid to landowners spilled over into a civil war that lasted a decade and claimed up to 15,000 lives. Talks to reopen the mine are ongoing causing significant concerns from the landholders. Opened 1972, closed 1989.

and controlled the people and the traffic going in and out of Arawa. The rebels were nowhere to be seen, as they were crawling through the jungle, but most mixed around with the ordinary Bougainvillean people and the soldiers were truly suspicious of everyone. I was fearful of the soldiers with their powerful guns that they slung across their heavily uniformed selves.

One weekend my father came and picked me to go and spend the weekend in our village Oria and I saw all the checkpoints for the soldiers that we had to go through. It was real scary shit and I didn't like it one bit.

Cheryl and I did our practical and we lived with Mr. and Mrs. Barry, who were very kind and took good care of us. When our practical period was over, the school and parents organised a picnic at Ako beach and we all went there and had a lovely time. They presented us with a huge cake and a lot of other gifts.

We went back to College and finished off the year in high spirits.

Finally, graduation day came and the College came alive with bustling activities.

My mother, Margaret Potoura came for the big day, plus my aunty Mary and her family, aunty Ruth and her family and my matrilineal grandmother Roandi Kauva, who lived with aunty Mary during that time.

After I marched down the aisle with my paper in my hand, I joined the queue of graduands and everyone congratulated us. My family and friends put leis around my shoulders and gave me gifts, as they shook my hands and kissed me on my cheeks.

Later Aunty Mary held my hand and we walked to her car.

'This is for you' she said pointing to a large colourful gift all wrapped up nicely. I tore the wrappers and there in front of me, in its own zipped bag carrier was a synthetic doona, like the ones she had in her home. But this one was orangey, with tiger like stripes and was unbelievably large. I hugged my aunty and kissed her. "Oh, thank you so much aunty, since high school you have taken really good care of me. You are truly wonderful."

'Well' she said, "you might go back home to Bougainville and get married, then that doona will be doubly useful." We both laughed loudly.

Aunt Mary holds a special place in my heart, as she played a pivotal role in guiding me through the intricacies of navigating the civilised world during my high school and college years in East New Britain Province. She instilled in me the values and customs essential for thriving in modern society, imparting her wisdom and experience with steady dedication.

Aunt Mary was not just an ordinary Papua New Guinean; she epitomized a unique blend of modernity and tradition. Her lifestyle surpassed the norms, as evidenced by her ownership of the esteemed Ocean Park in Kokopo and her residence of a luxurious high-class home.

Her unexpected passing in 2022 left me reeling, unprepared and unwilling to accept the harsh reality of her absence. The profound loss of Aunt Mary continues to weigh heavily on my heart, a wound that time has yet to heal.

The doona that Aunt Mary gifted me was truly a divine blessing, a thoughtful gesture that reflected the kindness and generosity embedded in her heart. It felt as though the benevolent hand of the Lord guided her to bestow such a precious gift upon me, a gesture that would later evoke overwhelming gratitude in my heart.

From that moment on, Aunt Mary held a sacred place at the core of my being, her presence shaping my life in ways I could never have imagined. Her sudden departure from this world dealt a devastating blow, a loss so profound that coming to terms with it remains an ongoing struggle. The void left by her absence is a constant reminder of the profound impact she had on my life, a testament to the enduring bond we shared.

I packed all my gifts and my belongings, farewelled all my college friends and with my mother and all my relatives, left for aunty Mary's house in Rabaul town. Aunty cooked a special meal and we ate together as mother related the tension and happenings in Bougainville. My grandmother Roandi started crying, as she thought of all her children, her husband Kauva and relatives back home.

After spending a few days at Aunt Mary's home, my mother and I bid farewell to our relatives, shedding a few extra tears as we embraced each other and wept. We boarded the plane and flew to Aropa airport, where my father awaited us. He greeted us warmly and drove us to our village of Oria.

My father had another awesome present waiting for me. He made me close my eyes and led me upstairs to our house. Then we walked around the house for a bit and he told me to open my eyes. There was a door in front of me and he urged me to open it. I opened it and there was a lovely room, with a bed all made up and a shelf for my books. I was overly thrilled.

'Oh, thank you, papa,' I yelled and hugged him, while my mother and siblings looked on and smiled. My father had turned the spare room, where we kept all the clothes and extra beddings into a lovely room for me.

'You are grown up now. You need a room for yourself,' he told me.

He even built a veranda on the other side of the house with better ladder and steps, while my room was now at the back of the house.

Great, now I didn't have to sleep with my little sister Linda on our bunker beds. My legs were now too long and didn't fit, so the room father built for me was awesome and I loved it.

In 1990, I got a teaching job at Hairu Adventist school. It was truly awesome, as this was the school I did my grades 1-6 at. And the Headmaster, was my grade one teacher, Mr. Timothy Ambi.

My initial year of teaching proved to be a significant challenge, to say the least. Struggling to maintain a facade of confidence, I encountered a multitude of issues that greatly impacted my journey. Foremost among these challenges was my youthfulness at just 20 years old, coupled with a lack of practical experience and an abundance of theoretical classroom knowledge that failed to prepare me adequately for the realities I faced. Teaching a grade 5 class comprised mainly of students from Oria and Paghui, who happened to be my own relatives, presented a unique set of hurdles.

Communication posed a major obstacle as the students predominantly conversed in their native language, making it difficult for me to conduct lessons in English. This language barrier often left me feeling frustrated and self-conscious, especially when met with snickers or remarks in our mother tongue during class. While the students attempted to demonstrate respect, I found myself grappling with a deep-seated desire to earn their genuine regard, a feat that seemed elusive at the time.

In addition to my lack of experience and occasional immaturity, I struggled with maintaining control and discipline within the classroom. While my teaching methods and ability to motivate the students were adequate, the challenge of enforcing order and managing disruptive behaviour proved to be a formidable task. Moreover, I found the assertiveness of some male students to be particularly overwhelming, their strong-willed nature adding another layer of complexity to an already demanding environment.

There was a boy from Paghui village, a relative of mine, who proved to be quite a source of frustration and concern for me. His behaviour often kept me up at night, filled with worry and anxiety. This headstrong and troublesome individual (may he rest in peace) had a knack for pushing my limits. Whenever I reprimanded him in class for neglecting his work, his response was met with piercing glares and the forceful slamming of doors or even striking the walls with a stick outside the classroom. This disruptive behaviour forced me to tread carefully, regardless of whether he was completing his assignments or not.

Furthermore, rumours circulated among my cousins, who were also students in my class, suggesting that this boy exhibited signs of mental instability. Much to my dismay, these claims were proven true sooner than I had anticipated, adding another layer of complexity to an already challenging situation.

During a math lesson one morning, as the clock approached 9:30 am in a school day that typically commenced at 8:00 am, I was engrossed in teaching long multiplication and division to the class. Suddenly, a deafening bang reverberated against the classroom wall, jolting us all from our focus. I reacted swiftly and dashed outside, with my cousin Jacob Mosina closely following behind. When I swung open the door, we were met by the sight of the culprit standing there, brandishing a massive stick in a threatening manner. Jacob wasted no time in admonishing him to cease his disruptive actions.

Jacob and I were enraged by the disturbance and I confronted the individual, questioning his motives for striking the classroom walls and causing a commotion that had unsettled everyone. In a heated exchange, he justified his actions by claiming that he had knocked on the door and been ignored, a blatant falsehood given his tardiness. As tension escalated, he struck the wall with his stick, prompting a chorus of screams from the classroom before he began to retreat.

I trailed after him, as I was driven by a mixture of concern and determination, towards the rear of the classroom, while Jacob cautioned me in our shared language to exercise caution, labelling the boy as disturbed. As I persisted in my pursuit, I found myself face-to-face with a chilling moment as he abruptly turned towards me, wielding a sharp knife in his grasp. Fear gripped me as I braced for the worst, closing my eyes in anticipation of an imminent attack. To my relief, he halted just inches away from me before abruptly fleeing down the road, leaving a lingering sense of unease in his wake.

Teaching at that school during those turbulent times was truly unsettling. It seemed as though a collective madness had taken hold of the boys, transforming them into a semblance of characters from a dramatic blockbuster film, with the Bougainville Crisis serving as their twisted script. The atmosphere was charged with tension as these troubled youths began to exhibit erratic behaviour, some going as far as bringing knives to school.

The grim reality was that many of these boys eventually succumbed to the allure of rebellion, abandoning their education to join the ranks of the insurgents. They traded textbooks for homemade water pipe guns, becoming embroiled in a conflict that seemed to consume all facets of their young lives.

In 1990 the people from the coastal villages started moving inland to Oria and Paghui villages and sought refuge with our people inland. The PNG soldiers were patrolling the waters and causing havoc to most of the villages because they couldn't spot the rebels anywhere.

The children in class, especially the boys' heads, were already muddled up by the crisis. If I scolded them in class for not doing their work, they retaliated with different means. Once they broke into my classroom and wrote very bad cuss words on the blackboard. I told the Head master and it sort of fell on deaf ears. I told my parents and they didn't react the way I had expected. I was so angry I didn't go to teach and went over to my cousin Kiatui's house and told her what had happened. She ignited the fire in me and both of us were totally over heated. I told her that we should leave Oria and go to Tugiogu, which is my mother's village, around two days walk away.

During that time, the roads were not safe, as most rebels were okay, but others were a bunch of trouble makers. We walked to Leulo and as we went past our bubu Kaveri's house, she called out to us in a very concerned voice and asked where we were going. We hurried by and told her we were going to a Youth camp at Iviro and the pickup truck would pick us up from the highway. She was still yelling for more information as we hurried away. We climbed up Mt Sansaro and when we saw people or heard the sound of vehicles, we hid in the bushes. It was a long climb up and finally, we reached the summit and looked across the Telei valley. It was breathtaking and beautiful.

We slowly walked down with our knees wobbling and arrived in Turutai village. Our very close relatives lived right next to the main road and they were my father's aunty Mevaki's family. Mevaki was Potoura's sister and she got married to a man from Turutai. We crept around the road, hiding from our uncles Boua and Kamaro, as they might see us and question us about where we were off to. Any sane person on the highway would be overly curious and suspicious of two young women walking with bags on their shoulders and furtively looking back and front. It was very obvious to us too, that we were running away from home.

We arrived at Tuvau hamlet as dusk was falling and went to aunt Gwen's house (may she rest in peace). She served us dinner, prepared our beds, and we spent a restless night there. I vividly recall our sleeplessness, even feeling frightened by the hooting of an owl that night.

Very early the next morning, we awoke and assisted aunt Gwen in cooking breakfast, which consisted of fried bananas, and we reheated the smoked fish over the hot charcoals. After eating together, we shook hands with aunt Gwen and her husband, expressing our gratitude for their hospitality, and then we resumed our journey.

The sun came up and the Buin highway was scorching. We kept ducking into drains and running into the bushes, when we saw people and heard vehicles. We arrived at Loubai river and decided to go under the bridge and have a swim. We swam in the cool crystal river, ate our food that aunty Gwen had packed for us and rested for a little while.

Then we started walking again and as we rounded the next bend, without warning, my aunty Lucia and her husband Rughakei came around the corner and we didn't have time to flee. Lucia was from Tugiogu and she was the one I used to go out with and collect sago grubs when I was young child of around 7 years old. She was now married to Rughakei who was from Perai village, where we were about to pass as we walked on the Buin to Arawa highway.

Lucia had a lot to say and forced us to go with her to Perai, as Rughakei shook his head in fear and confusion and followed us. When we went to Perai, Rughakei told us that walking on the highway was not safe, so he would take us to Tugiogu through the bush road. We left Lucia and walked with Rughakei through Kikimohu and crossed Siribai and Porou rivers and then it started to rain.

Rughakei cut the wild banana leaves and gave to us for cover from the rain and we walked in the mud and the puddles. My legs ached like crazy and to make things worse, Rughakei was walking too fast and Kiatui and I were really complaining.

Finally, we arrived in Iviro village around 6:30pm and then we walked to Tugiogu and arrived there around 7:30pm. Uncle Donald and his wife Mary were truly confused and surprised to see us, but welcomed us with open arms and gave us a hot supper of coconut cream fish and mumu tapiok.

The next day, my brother Kiason and Kiatui's brother Kokinai both arrived at Tugiogu and told us that my father will come for us and put the axe on our heads for not letting our parents know where we were going, risking our lives and walking on the dangerous main highway. I wasn't scared, because I was in my mother's village and my uncles would protect us, if truly father was going to come with the tomahawk.

Father came a few days later and picked us up in his vehicle. He didn't say a word, but when Kiatui and I arrived in Oria, everyone wanted to know how we walked the long road to Tugiogu. We told the story over and over and soon we were pretty proud of ourselves.

As our village, Oria, was inundated with people fleeing from the coastal villages, teaching at Hairu became increasingly challenging. The boys arrived at school with a variety of defiant attitudes, and I harboured fears of the slingshots and knives they concealed in their trousers.

I continued to teach the students without receiving any wages, striving to educate my relatives and the others who attended Hairu school.

Eventually, I persuaded my parents to allow me to live at the school, a mere ten-minute walk away. I was yearning for independence and self-reliance. Initially, my parents objected, but they relented after my persistent sulking. With their approval, I moved to reside at the school.

Many of my cousins joined me, and we settled into a newly constructed house, donated by the logging company, TDC – Tonolei Development Corporation.

The students at Hairu school, mostly my relatives, brought me fresh produce from their gardens every day. In Oria, food is abundant; our valley's high fertility ensures that gardens flourish with ease.

2
War rages in Bougainville
'Bloodlines disrespected and destroyed'

We started hearing stories about rebels. Well, actually they came under the name rebels, militants, rambos, BRA (Bougainville Revolutionary Army), these were the common names they were known by. We heard that they were coming to homes in the dark of the night and getting shot guns and 22's from men whom they knew possessed registered guns.

Well, the stories proved to be true, because one night they came to our house. I woke up in the middle of the night and heard muffled voices downstairs. I crept silently into my parent's bedroom, but the beds were empty. I stood at the top of the stairs and realised the lantern was on downstairs. I rubbed my eyes and then I had the shock of my life.

There were people with guns all over our lawn and even two were sitting on our steps. I looked downstairs and saw my father talking to a man. A short, stout, muscular man. Mother was sitting next to dad as well. Father and the man were deep in conversation. It looked like a very interesting conversation.

I know my father was totally into Bougainville breaking away from PNG, so I went back into the house and slept. In the morning, I asked father what was going on and he said, "those people who came last night are the ones truly fighting for the breakaway of Bougainville from Papua New Guinea."

I asked what they wanted and he said that "they asked him to sign his guns out." I had a very bad feeling about that and continued to ask, "what were they going to do with the guns."

Father explained that they needed the guns for protection because PNG was declaring war soon.

Father's guns were licensed for hunting only.

The rebels started dropping by in my village and harassing the villagers. They would come just before dawn, and start firing guns and waking every one up. The kids would start crying at suddenly being awoken and the men would get together to face the rebels and see what they were after.

The woman would sit together and try to keep the children quiet. The rebels would harass and hit the men right in front of our eyes. I couldn't understand why brothers were harassing the ones who did not hold any weapons. These were very confusing times to me.

As we continued to hear mortars thrown in distant villages by the PNG army, there were militants with guns who also came and physically harassed my father and took his Hilux away. This created so much anger in me. I couldn't understand why our own people on the island were harassing their own, while we stood together to protect our lands.

I believe that showed my father that not everyone was genuine and there were already opportunists who were taking the crisis for granted and harassing their own people.

Father also had to retrieve most of my uncles' household belongings that were left behind when they fled Bougainville. With mother they hired two big trucks to rescue what they could.

I remember a day we had to continue to retrieve belongings from our uncles houses and even their vehicles were left behind. It felt like the end of the world where everyone fled and abandoned all their household wealth.

Father also retrieved three of my uncle's vehicles and there was a time we were on one of the Toyota Hilux, he was driving home and as we turned the Koromira corner, the engine died as the battery gave way. We kept pushing and helping father to make it start but the engine was dead.

An hour later, a group of militants with guns, came driving by and stopped, asking father what was going on. I thought they were going to get the vehicle off father, but they helped jumpstart the battery and the engine came alive and we were on our way.

I only remember my father's Hilux, which some rascal militants took on that rainy day and to be truthful, they kept on driving that Hilux even after the war. All the other vehicles that father had, plus the ones he retrieved from the uncle's home, I am not sure what happened to them. I cannot remember right now.

As the situation continued to deteriorate, my father ventured into one of his cocoa plantations and constructed a shed at its centre. This shed served as a fortified warehouse, reinforced with corrugated iron and raised half a metre above the ground on timber from his sawmill. It featured a substantial wooden door secured by a sizeable chain lock. We contributed to the project in every way we could, ensuring the structure was well-concealed beneath the plantation's foliage to avoid detection.

He gathered us all and told us to select our most cherished belongings, pack them neatly into bags, and carry them to the shed on the cocoa plantation. I placed my Mills and Boon books, Harlequin novels, the "Flowers in the Attic" series, and 'Strange Case of Dr Jekyll & Mr Hyde' novel into an old suitcase. I securely packed my doona into its special zippered bag and nestled it inside my mother's chest, alongside all her household blankets. The shed became quite crowded due to the numerous items my mother had removed from our house in the village.

"Houses are being torched by both the militants and the PNG soldiers in the early hours of the mornings. When they come to our village, vacate the house and flee to Soro," he instructed us. "Do not go to the shed until the war is over," he finished off and gave the shed key to mother. The Soro hideout refuge was on one of his lands that him and mother had prepared beforehand, when the crisis had started.

Father leaves for Rabaul (1991&1992)

Between 1990 to 1992 significant events happened in my family and extended families.

Due to PNG army withdrawal from Bougainville, two main things happened.

First, Bougainville was in a total blockade from PNG and the outside world. Second, a deliberate setting of Bougainvilleans against each other on geographic or ethnic lines. This went on for a while and then the blockage thinned out and ships started bringing vital goods to Kangu wharf.

Thinking all was going to be well, my father and other landowner spokesmen, left for Rabaul to sort out the TDC logging royalties for the landowners.

When father left, it was not long until the blockade worsened, due to tough BRA activities all around the coastal areas of Bougainville. PNG Defence force's lack of interest to get back on the island where the BRAs were attacking with force, was not what the withdrawal of the forces in the first place intended. It was the planners' intention that from the army's withdrawal and the blockade, Bougainvilleans would fight against each other and lead to the collapse of the BRA within months.

During this time, the blockade led to the division within the creation of the so-called resistance forces, which were seen as armed and financed by the Papua New Guinea Defence Force and Australian Defence Force. It was also during this time that BRA extended its influence over all of Bougainville and Buka Island.

Ethnic and tribal conflict also surfaced and BRAs, Militants and Rebels, utilised the internecine period to settle old scores.

As the conflict continued, significant events happened in my immediate family and extended families, that has been etched in my mind.

One of my uncles, whose house was on the next hill, opposite Hairu School where I was teaching, was torched by the militants and he was taken away. His whereabouts enquiries were filled with confusing stories and he was never returned to our village and to his family. In 2008, I escorted an aunt from Port Moresby and we brought a coffin home to our village because reliable sources had informed his younger brothers, where his body was. We went home with the coffin and my uncles retrieved and placed him in the coffin and buried him in our village cemetery in Oria. He was a well-known wealthy business man, whose life was shortened without a trial. To this day, I have no idea, why his life was ended.

While father was in Rabaul, the blockade on Bougainville caused so many people to suffer under the rule of the militants.

Oria village was labelled as anti –BRA, supporting the PNG soldiers. To this day, I still cannot understand, the atrocities of the Bougainville Crisis over the people of Oria. My people, before the crisis, were the most industrious and no nonsense indigenous of the land. Even now, after the crisis, though blood was drawn upon our land, by torturing and assassinating my people by the so-called militants, the Orians have regained their wealth and prosperity as I write. If they must prosper upon their land, they will continue to do so. What God has given and blessed; no men shall remove.

As the war raged on, my father was not with us, and he was listed as a suspect. The militants continued to harass my family because of their suspicions. Due to their horrendous activities among their own people, the name BRA faded away, and we started calling them militants

We kept on fleeing into the forests, in fear of the militants and the PNG soldiers. At that time, I was confused which side was genuine. This made me really hate the war and I was totally fed up of being hungry in the bushes hiding from both the militants and the soldiers.

Our fleeing was quite funny, as at times, we would get fed up and go back to our house in the village and then one of my uncles would come and tell us to leave the village and go to our hiding place to avoid any unpleasant encounter with the BRAs or the PNG soldiers.

Sometime later, we were told to move back to our village as instructed by word from the militants.

In the early hours of the morning, I heard a fierce knock on my door and my mother yelling, 'open the door' and with sleepy eyes, I turned the lock and strange men rushed into my room, looking for a wireless or something that they said, my father using to contact PNG soldiers.

I recognised them, as men from the next village who were much stronger now because rifles ruled and even today, I am still confused which were the BRAs, Militants and just overall trouble makers.

That day started gloomy with dark clouds across the skies. All the men in Oria were told to go to the youth hall in the centre of the village and be questioned. Suspicion was on my father over guns that were believed to have been shipped before the crisis and were buried on his land in one of his cacao plantations. As the rain fell, the thunder rolled and lightning streaked across the darkened sky, my brothers were told (they were quite young) to lead the way into the cacao plantations in search of the buried guns, as the militants supervised them under rifle order.

No guns were found.

Beloved Papa (1993)

As we closed off 1992, my village Oria was a marked village, in the sense that militants had this constant belief that my people were dealing with the PNG Defence Force.

One of the reasons was that there were a lot of half-caste PNG people in Oria. And also, when the BRAs took over, old feuds were ignited by the ones with guns and therefore, had dominion over the ones without.

That was when the great pain hit me that my father was under serious suspicion.

And it was during this time that my heart was heavy and I was deeply troubled, worried sick over my father. There were times, when I would just cry, missing my father so much and didn't know what to do. I heard stories of prestigious men, chiefs, leaders and professionals, who were taken out of their homes and never returned to see their families. I was lost and miserable.

My family, extended family and my father's tribal clan heard about my state of being; worried about my father and always weeping for him. They would come and encourage me that everything was going to be alright. But there was a deep gnawing sadness, I felt back then, which I still have not experienced again.

Somehow, word reached my father in Rabaul that I was always crying for him and when one of the men who went with him, somehow returned, through the Solomon Islands, to Buin, father sent with him a letter to me. That was the last letter I ever received from my dear father and I still have it.

When I got out of Bougainville in 1993 December, my uncle Kia, who my father stayed with when he went to Rabaul, they were friends since those Irinioku days when they were teenagers, told me that when father was living with them, he was worried sick about us and had a stomach ulcer, because he was not eating and was under unbelievable stress.

One time, word came to us to move out of the village again. At around 4pm, we left the village and went into the forest lands. In Bougainville by 4pm, dusk is already creeping in. Mother instructed that we'd go and pitch our tents beneath the Wukomai mountain, which was next to one of our gardens.

As soon as we pitched our two tents, it started raining heavily. We sat huddled up in our tents, my younger sister and I in the smaller tent, hungry and cold, our coconut oil lamp burning with a dull glow, as we breathed in the essence of coconut, trying to quench our hunger.

Suddenly, the water from the mountain started cascading down, right into our tents, soaking the thin mats we laid on. I had to let my sister curl up on the less soaked part of the mat, while I stood outside of the tent, as the creek Wuloli swelled up, with all the extra water overrunning its banks.

I stood there, staring into the darkness, below the mountains, until dawn.

That was when it hit me; I was a fugitive, and numerous times I had taken refuge in the forest, in fear of the militants.

Yes, I was a fugitive, without a proper home anymore and I was sad. Will I ever see civilisation again? Will I live like this until I lose my life? That night, I experienced a deep, gnawing hunger; the kind that can only be appeased by a specific food that one craves.

Then, a wave of anger consumed me, making me acutely aware that I was utterly tired of consuming kaukau and banana, and yearning instead for a meal of chips and chicken accompanied by a refreshing can of coke.

I stood outside the tent, allowing my imagination to run wild, daydreaming about the books, comics, and the fast food I longed for in that moment.

As the orangey sun peeped through the towering trees, the nightmare of sleeplessness was quickly transcended by the beautiful Wuloli creek and the lush forest lands.

Mother urged us to fold the tents, advising us to cast aside the night's events from our minds. She reminded us that there were individuals in Bougainville grappling with tribulations far greater than ours, suggesting a perspective of resilience and gratitude amidst our own challenges.

We silently packed our tents and crossed the now rushing Wuloli creek, powered by the new flood and walked through the damp forest lands to a house, which my uncle had built for his plantation workers.

My mother is not from Oria and she didn't really like the idea of taking us into the forest lands. I believe she wanted my father to lead the way because it was his land and he would show us the right places to hide, as there were traditional stories of certain places not allowed for outsiders to set foot on.

We moved to the quaint little house and it offered a peaceful retreat far superior to the dense confines of the surrounding forests. It was perched at the edge of the cocoa plantation, atop a gentle hill overlooking the serene Wuloli creek from which we sourced our water.

When we lived at the plantation house, I was not the same as before. I was done.

That restless night spent at the base of the Wukomai mountain, under dense trees, left me utterly drained, prompting a profound realisation that I no longer desired to endure such discomfort. It ignited within me a burning desire to break free from the confines of my current existence and venture out into the vast world beyond. I was truly exasperated.

I found myself increasingly irritable, snapping at others and incessantly grumbling about the tedious and seemingly pointless chores that I was burdened with. I grew weary of constantly living in hiding, feeling as though we were no better than wild animals.

Honestly, I was at my wits end.

Reflecting on that moment in time, I now understand that deep within me, an intuitive sense forewarned of an impending, massive and heart-wrenching event on the horizon. A profound unease gripped me, foreshadowing the turmoil that lay ahead.

After a heated and intense argument with my mother, I silently slipped away from the plantation house under the cover of darkness, made my way back to the village in solitude.

During that time, everyone was terrified of going back to their villages, because militants were moving around occupying deserted villages. I didn't tell anyone, that I was going back to the village, though I was scared of the militants, I was tired, fed up and didn't really care.

There was no one in my village, so I crept into our house, opened the doors with my keys, got into the house and locked all the doors again. It was already after 7pm when I got into our house. I lay down on my comfortable mattress. I was pretty much tired from the turmoil of running in circles on our own land. I couldn't work out the root problem and the load of worrying was too much on my shoulders. As soon as my head touched the pillow, I was asleep.

I slept soundly through the night and only realised that it was raining when I woke up around 3:30am and listened for a while to the sound of the rain, as it pelted outside. I dozed off until the early hours of the morning.

Around 5am, I was suddenly woken up by sounds of heavy feet walking, dragging seats downstairs and the stomping of boots. I was alerted all at once and sat right up and listened. I heard the crickets and the morning birds, untamed songs, weakened by the night downpour. I was actually petrified and shaken, knowing militants were about to burn the house down and were creeping about downstairs. Again, I heard the sound of heavy feet walking on the concrete under our high stilted house, moving the wooden long seats and calling out, 'Laii, toheupi' (Hey, it's dawn).

I shot straight up, my heart pounding wildly, and listened. The crickets and the morning birds' weak songs with the drizzling showers, made the mood darker, as I sat there petrified, knowing the militants move around in the early hours of the morning.

I imagined the flames closing in on our house, threatening to engulf it first due to its position at the edge of the village. As I desperately prayed for a miracle, a familiar voice broke through my fear - my father's. I stood up, shaken to my core, wondering if this was the end for me and if my father was somehow reaching out to me from beyond. The terror of the situation caused my heart to race uncontrollably, my head filled with a frantic heat as I realised the grim reality that I was on the brink of being consumed by the flames.

'Sahela,' my father's voice called out my ancestral name once more, cutting through the haze of fear and confusion clouding my mind. I shook my head vigorously, attempting to dispel the oppressive heat that muddled my thoughts. His voice echoed again, compelling me to action. Without a moment's hesitation, I bolted out of the room, flung open the heavy main door, and descended the steps with legs trembling from days of hunger.

And there he was, my dear beloved father, waiting right at the end of the steps. I sprinted from the third last step and jumped onto his open arms sobbing my heart out. I heard him sniffing too and knew that he was crying. We stood in embrace and I lost count of the minutes. I felt safe and warm though he was soaked to the skin from the forest rains that he had endured, walking from the beach where he was left by a vessel, to our village.

It was the last time I hugged my father and the memory has been carved in my heart forever.

His big arms around me, comforted and erased all the fears and tension that I had felt earlier, the thoughts of militants burning me alive in our house. Till today, I still cannot work out how when I needed him the most, he came just to hug me and then was gone forever.

My father's last hug, is the most precious treasure, I have today. It is the sweetest memory he left behind, and I use that to cover up all the horrible things that happened to me during the crisis in Bougainville.

After our long, tearful hug, he asked me where everyone was and I told him that Oria people did not live in the village anymore; they were hiding in their garden huts or were in the forest lands because of the militants. I also told my father that it was not safe and that he had to return to Rabaul, because prominent indigenous people were being killed without questions and our Island home had become a very dangerous zone.

My father told me, he knew about the danger but he was now back home to his land, where he belonged. No one would do anything to him.

'Sahela, this is my land, my home, these are my people and I have returned,' father told me with so much confidence in his voice.

Those words have rung in my ears and I have never forgotten them. Because, it was not to be as he so strongly believed.

Father had gained a lot of weight in Rabaul after no physical activity and the long walk he had endured from *Turau*, up to our village Oria was tiring. He carried a large mountain bag on his back and a smaller one on the front and his boots were slung over his shoulders. I helped him carry his boots and we went up the stairs and into my room.

He changed his clothes and then told me that he was overly tired and was going to rest and sleep. He told me to go to our hideout and tell mother and everyone to come and see him. But before I left, he opened the large mountain bag and gave me so many gifts; a gold watch, a world receiver radio and rice, oh that was the best sight to behold. Rice! I saw rice and tinned fish and couldn't believe my eyes.

I was so tired of eating kaukau and edible bush leaves.

As father lay down to rest, I grabbed the rice, went to the thatched kitchen and tried to start a fire. There was no match to ignite a fire so I tried the traditional way of starting a fire. I sat against a stronger wood and start rubbing another smaller piece of stick, grasped in-between my palms. When the friction caused smoke, I quickly placed the dried coconut fibres on top and not long later I had a fire blazing. I placed the pot on the fire and sat around it cooking green bananas I had pulled down from the banana patch behind the kitchen.

Not long later, my brother and cousin brother, came around the corner, stealthily looking for me. I yelled at them and they came and sat beside the fire. They told me that the family found out in the morning that I was missing. I smiled and told them that I have great news. They asked what it was and I whispered to them that father had arrived and was sleeping in my room. They didn't believe the news and thought that I had 'lost' it, because of what I was going through lately.

No, I told them, "Papa is here. I am not lying, he is sleeping." I pulled the lid off the pot and they saw the rice cooking. Even before I placed the lid back, my brother and cousin raced up the steps to my room and saw father sleeping.

The three of us had the finest meal, eating rice and tinned fish after close to three years of kaukau and banana, without salt, flavoured with bush leaves.

Father had arrived during the blockade.

I know that father arrived on a Friday and the next day was Saturday and our closest family members like my uncle Amos (may his generous and loving self-RIP) came and saw father, after the Saturday worship.

I cannot remember the exact days and dates but I believe that father arrived home on the Friday, the 13th August 1993.

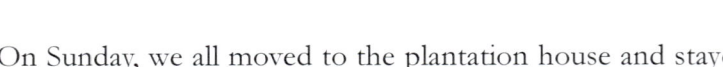

On Sunday, we all moved to the plantation house and stayed there. This plantation house, I keep mentioning, belonged to an uncle who had long fled Bougainville and was somewhere in PNG.

On the third day, father told mother to take us, his daughters, plus some other smaller cousins and an aunt, to the second hide out at Soro (name of the land in my Oria dialect) which was deep in the jungle along the Pirasi River on his land - where he hunted when he was a teenager. He loved this land so much and he would never let any other relatives make gardens or chop down the great trees that grew there. He was very firm about this and told us that it was proper and that he would come with the boys in the morning.

So as the sun set over the trees, we all gathered our few belongings into small bags and mother led the way and we started walking through the cacao trees. As we were about to go down the hill, father came over and repeated again that the boys and he would come to us in the morning.

Mother didn't know that that was the last time she would ever see or hear her husband again.

Father and the boys, plus two of my uncles and some cousins stayed on at the plantation house.

We went down the hill, crossed Wuloli creek and then into the jungle. The trees were very tall and the forest was already dark. Mother led the way along the narrow track, camouflaged by the protruding humps of roots that lay above the surface of the ground. The long vines that hung on the trees looked like serpents waiting to drop down and devour us.

I stumbled over the roots and lifted my skinny legs higher. The jungle sounded of sleepy birds and animals. We were terrified and deafened by the crickets. But our real fear was the rebels, who lurked in the forests on our island, Bougainville.

Mother kept hurrying us along, telling us to keep up. Aunty took out one of the dried coconut fronds she had packed in her knapsack and lit it with mother's matches. The fire made menacing shadows that danced beside us as we hurried. We had no words to complain, we had only to flee, as father had instructed.

I walked at the back and saw auntie's fire blowing sparks out into the darkness. I was afraid to look behind me, as that would be a bad omen. Looking back and blinking would be beckoning the forest ghouls to follow.

Finally, we heard the rumble of river Pirasi. Aunty held the fire higher and we saw why mother had stopped. The old mother tree, known as Moileu in our mother tongue, was right in our path. I knew about Moileu, as I had heard that my father's ancestors held sacred gatherings under it, to call the mighty wind. We walked around her huge trunk, as Moileu stood in silence.

When we arrived at our hide-out, aunty quickly built a fire in the thatch roofed hut and we warmed our bodies; shivering not from the cold but from immense fear. Mother, who was asthmatic, was wheezing badly. My cousin Lorna and I fixed up her treasured tent next to our bush hut, while aunty looked for leaves to warm over the fire and put on mother's chest. Afterwards, when she felt a little better, we helped her into her tent and made her comfortable by the light of the coconut oil lamp.

Then we all laid down in a line on the wild bush palm leaves in the hut and as the embers glowed, we went to sleep. I woke up early, maybe around 5am, a normal time to wake up in Bougainville because the sun rises early on our island.

But because we were in the forest, the place was still dark. I lay cold and frightened as the sound of the morning birds came cackling, sounding weirdly unnatural. I can still remember the goose bumps that crept up my bare feet, like crawling ants. I shook my aunty awake and told her that I was scared my mother might have died in her tent and if she could please go and check.

Aunty came back and told me that mother was okay and then we sat there, building up the fire and conversing in hushed voices.

I went outside the hut and sat on a log and watched sunbeams dancing to the rustling tune of the leaves. Day time brought the beauty of the forest. I saw how peaceful and untouched everything was. The tree trunks came in different colours, with vines that wrapped around them and also hung in mid-air like swings.

There were shrubs, ferns and other smaller trees growing everywhere on the forest floor. I saw so many birds flying from branch to branch, all busy eating seeds. Their cries, shrieks, cackles and songs were now sweet and soothing to my ears. I heard the river Pirasi rumbling nearby and then looked back into the hut and saw Aunty cooking green bananas over the open fire, while her 6-year-old son Robin and my 4-year-old brother David sat near her.

I saw my sister and our cousins listening to the soft music on my radio. I can still remember the song that was on. It was the **'Warrior of love.'**

Suddenly, we were surrounded by strange men who crept around our hut. I saw them first, because I was outside the hut. Dangerous looking men, who had dreadlocks, while others covered their heads with leaves, bandanas and woollen caps. They wore worn out attire and had bare feet.

They held shot guns and other home-made guns, which were made out of water pipes and didn't have safety catches, and went off anytime without warning.

They were dragging my 16-year-old cousin Kerosi by the cuff of his old shirt. They had captured him to show them the way. They searched roughly through our hut and woke my mother in her tent. She came out looking quite ill. They seized my world service portable mini radio, claiming that it was a wireless to call the Papua New Guinea soldiers.

As they searched our hut, Kerosi quietly related to me that my father and everyone had been taken by the rebels as prisoners and were badly beaten up. The men then yanked my cousin from where we were standing and disappeared into the thick jungle.

My aunty and mother started weeping. We were all shocked and didn't know what to do. I told them that I was going back to the plantation house to confirm Kerosi's story.

I walked back stealthily through the lush untouched forest lands. Moileu started whooshing and creaking as I crept past her gigantic trunk. I walked on and at last came through thinner jungle to arrive at the village gardens. I crossed Wuloli creek and then I went up the hill. I slowed my pace and crept to the plantation house.

There was no one there.

The house had been torn apart by people who were mad with anger and in a wild tantrum. All our things in the house were scattered everywhere, stamped on, broken to pieces and butted with guns. I saw blood all around the steps and underneath the house as well.

My head reeled and I held onto the post of the house for a few minutes, until I caught my balance again. I decided to walk on to our village Oria and see if there was anyone there. I walked through the cacao trees and came to the village along a small unknown track.

All the houses were abandoned. The whole village was deserted. Everyone had fled into the jungles.

I followed the main highway and tried to look for my beloved father and my two dear brothers. I slowly went down the hill and felt my legs wobbling, from uncertainty, fear and lack of food. I rounded the next corner and as I was about to cross the river Pauhu, I saw my father's step father Puriala, coming from the other direction. He was shaking and sobbing uncontrollably and his face, I saw, was disfigured from so much tension and worry.

We both stood there in the middle of the road and cried our hearts out. I can still remember what the old man said as he wept. "They've taken them all. They've tortured them and knifed them like animals and may have killed them already."

He held my hands with his shaking hands and told me to go back to my mother and flee further into the jungles. I ran back up the hill and on to the trail I had taken earlier. I shivered as I ran past the plantation house, then into the forest once again, now alive with noises of birds. I reached Moileu and this time, her branches were creaking and swaying wildly, as her leaves whistled to the wind.

I ran to our camp and there was no one there. Everything was packed and gone, only the bush hut was still there. I was terrified, realising the cool zephyr had now changed. The trees were swaying frantically to the wind that was gradually forming in the forest. I noticed the birds' songs turned to screeches, as they tried to seek shelter elsewhere.

I ran all the way back to the plantation house again and there I was held at gun point by another group of people from Paghui village, our neighbouring relatives. The group was led by a relative of my father Tuvunau. He asked me where mother and them were and I told him that I was looking for them. They followed me into the forest lands with the gun raised, worried that I was taking them to PNG soldiers. "No", I told them, "I am going to look for mother and everyone I left in the forest".

They were right behind me stumbling over the many roots until we reached our campsite and there was no one there. I turned around and started going down the hill to the river Pirasi with the men following behind with their rifles raised. The river was clear and flowing fast. I stood on the rocky bank and observed the surroundings. Then I walked downstream for a good number of minutes, until I heard someone whistle our family's secret whistle.

I looked across and saw my mother, my aunty, my cousins, my brother and my sister Linda. I waded across the river and I ran to my family and hugged them all. We sat on the ferns on the forest floor and I related what I had encountered.

They looked across the river and saw Tuvunau and his group waiting for us.

That day, when my father was taken away by the militants, I found myself running through the forest in rage, an experience carved into my memory forever. The trees seemed to come alive, their rustling leaves forming an angry, frenzied chant that echoed around me. The forest itself appeared different, almost sentient, as I dashed back and forth on that fateful 23rd of August.

It's a moment that defies explanation, a unique encounter that has shaped my understanding of nature on a deeply personal level. Only those who have undergone a similar trial can truly grasp the profound connection I felt with the living, breathing entities that surrounded me that day.

As Tuvunau's group escorted us back through the darkening forest, a sense of desolation and tragedy hung heavy in the air when we reached the plantation house. The sight of my mother and aunty softly weeping only added to the sombre atmosphere.

Guided by the men through the shadowy cacao trees, we eventually reached our house in the village. It was there that we were informed we would spend the night under their watchful eyes, with decisions about our fate to be made in the morning.

Reflecting on that harrowing night, I am filled with gratitude towards Tuvunau and his companions, knowing that our lives could have taken a much darker turn had they not intervened on our behalf.

That unforgettable night spent in our house remains fixed in my memory, as inexplicable events unfolded with the guards Tuvunau had stationed to watch over us until morning. We, along with my mother, aunty, and the children, decided to lay our beddings in the living room, opting not to use the bedrooms.

Sometime between 1:00 to 3:00 am, the eerie silence was shattered by the sound of the guards frantically running up the steps, their screams echoing through the house as they pounded on the front door. Startled from our sleep, we all awoke in a panic, joining in their cries of distress.

In the midst of the chaos, my mother swiftly retrieved the glowing coconut oil lamp from one of the rooms and hurried to the door, with the rest of us following closely behind. Upon opening the door, we were met with a chilling sight - three guards stood before us, trembling uncontrollably. The youngest among them bore a grotesquely swollen lower lip, protruding several inches out and marred with dark bruises, a haunting image that left us all bewildered and fearful.

"Please, help us, we are being terrorized by a large, shadowy figure that keeps changing its form and it struck me in the face," the younger guard stammered, his voice trembling with fear and disbelief.

Aunty swiftly retrieved a coconut oil lamp and positioned it on the veranda, casting a warm, flickering glow that illuminated the tensed faces of the men as they recounted their harrowing experience. Throughout the night, she sat with them, offering words of comfort and reassurance as the hours crept by until the first light of dawn broke through the darkness.

This inexplicable incident remains a mystery to me, a haunting memory that defies rational explanation. As morning arrived, the men departed without a word, leaving behind unanswered questions and a lingering sense of unease.

Amidst this bleak backdrop, one figure stood out in stark contrast - my father's first cousin, the kind-hearted uncle Kusivai, and his gracious wife Emilyn, may she rest in peace. Unlike the others, they did not simply pass by with a wave, but stopped to offer us a lifeline in the form of an abundance of garden produce. As Emilyn engaged us in conversation, uncle Kusivai sprang into action, disappearing briefly before remerging with a hefty piece of wood. With practiced efficiency, he set to work, chopping and stacking firewood next to our kitchen, ensuring that we had the means to cook and nourish ourselves during our time of need.

The simple yet profound act of kindness and generosity that uncle Kusivai displayed that day remains imprinted in my memory, a beacon of light in our darkest hour of hunger and sorrow.

As the week drew to a close, Tuvunau arrived with a grave expression on his face, bearing news that would alter the course of our lives once again. He informed us that we were to accompany him to a secluded hideout, where my father's uncle Kaleva and his family resided. Kaleva was my father's clansman, who was highly respected of the chieftan family.

We urgently farewelled aunty Aretai and her children, as they would be joining aunt's relatives, in their small hamlet along the Pirasi river. We hastily gathered our belongings once more, preparing for yet another journey into the unknown. The weight of uncertainty hung heavy in the air as we set out on that Friday, trudging alongside Tuvunau through the forest lands until we arrived at the hideout nestled beside a babbling small creek.

I can't remember the name of the place Tuvunau took us to, but the creek there was unforgettable. It was the smallest, coldest, and crystal-clear babbling creek I've ever seen. Its pristine beauty and soothing sound made it a magical experience that I will never forget.

We arrived at the hideout and didn't have much to say but everyone at the camp was kind and understanding. We sat there and stared into the rainforest and waited for each day to end. The people at the camp shared their little food with us, but most of the time, there was nothing to eat and we didn't complain. Elma Savu, a clan's woman of my father's, was very kind to us and I have never forgotten that. She has passed away now, but what a good heart she had. A lasting reminder of the kindness she showed.

After a day or so, mother decided to go to the plantation house and round up the chooks and ducks that she kept fenced up behind the large Okilo amongst the cacao trees.

Tuvunau escorted her with two of his guys and we walked through the forest lands to the plantation house. When we arrived, we realised that the fence was opened and the chooks and ducks were roaming freely in the cacao trees. Mother told us to chase them and catch as many as possible to share with our kin at the hideout. We ran through the cacao trees as the chickens clacked and tried to run fast but we caught them. The ducks were easier to catch as their webbed feet got tangled in the kominis vines.

We tied their legs together and collected a lot of eggs around the shades of trees, behind the stumps and in the grass. One funny thing I still remember now was Tuvunau making little holes in the eggs and sucking the yolk out raw. My sister and small brother were terribly horrified.

We lived in open huts constructed amidst the forest floor. They were partially enclosed with woven sago palms or bamboo. At night, our cousin Isabelle would snore, prompting Linda and me to gently shake her to silence. We slept on a long, wide bed crafted from torre, raised a metre above the ground.

Tuvunau's and Elma's family occupied one end, while we slept at the other end, our legs meeting in the middle. The occupants were Mother, Linda, cousin Isabelle, David, and myself. Linda was around 14 years old, Isabelle about 10, David 6, and I was 23.

One memorable night, we were all awakened by Betty's (RIP) screams from another hut about 15 to 20 metres from where we were, followed by Kaleva's loud voice demanding to know the reason for her screams.

Startled, we sat up as Tuvunau instructed us to remain calm while he investigated. Fear gripped me, thinking it was an impending attack on our bush camp. Mother advised us to hold onto our knapsacks, which we used as pillows. Before long, Tuvunau returned and explained that Betty had been screaming because she felt cold, freezing hands on her thighs, which we all concluded as an entity of some sort.

Tuvunau would depart from the campsite to his group of men, then embarking on exploratory missions to survey the Paghui and Oria villages, as well as the main highways, returning with vital updates for us.

I, too, ventured into the forest expanses, accompanied by Linda, Isabelle, and David. Our explorations led us through the dense woodlands, trekking for approximately 15 minutes until we reached the Pirasi River. Following its meandering course downstream for about an hour, we engaged in fishing with makeshift lines and foraged for edible wild leaves.

We arrived at aunty Aretai's hamlet, where her blind mother, our Bubu Lukumi, resided. We spent the day there, before bidding them farewell and retracing our steps upstream to return to our campsite.

Mother tried to discourage me from roaming and frolicking through the forest lands, but I couldn't bear to sit idly and await news of my father, brothers, and uncles. In our hearts, we held onto the belief that they were held captive at a camp in Tavatava, a village in central Bougainville under the watchful eyes of guards, surveillance, and interrogations.

This conviction fuelled our hope, and we remained optimistic about their imminent return.

Following their capture, no one provided us with any information. In hindsight, I realise that there were stories known to others, including Tuvunau and his group, yet they chose to shield us from the truth to spare us further distress. I believe they were biding their time, anticipating a specific moment, and eventually, that moment arrived.

One and a half weeks from the 23rd of August, on a gloomy rainy Thursday afternoon at around 6pm, Tuvunau came from his expeditions with tears in his eyes and told us that our father was found downstream at River Loluai, by a man and his son.

Rest in peace, my Papa
(1993 November)

My father was taken on the 23rd of August, and we received no confirmation of what had happened to him, my brothers, cousins, and uncles. For the past one to two weeks, we held onto the hope that they were all alive, but sadly, that was not the case. I wandered through the forest, clinging to the belief that my father was still alive.

The day I frantically traversed the forest was the very day my father was assassinated. The night when Tuvunau's men were terrorised by an unknown force was the same night my father's body lay in the Loluai River.

Imagine the overwhelming sense of brokenness I felt upon realising that my father had been dead for almost two weeks, and that my two uncles were already in their self-dug grave. What kind of atrocity can this assassination be classified as, for indigenous Bougainvilleans? Why?

As the terrible news unfolded before us, mother instructed us to gather our belongings and we walked to our village in the night, guided by the flickering light of an oil lamp.

When we arrived, we were met by aunty Aretai and some of her relatives who had already gathered and were waiting for us. People were emerging from their hideouts and moving into the village, and we could hear my father's closest kin wailing and lamenting as we approached.

Meanwhile, my father's relatives had heard stories that Ruaki, a respected man and my father's clans man from Wisau, was tirelessly scouring the Loluai River in search of my father's body, and they were anxiously awaiting any updates.

Before my father was killed, he was knifed through his abdomen. The oppression that my father endured and took humbly were related to me by an uncle who was made to stand beside my father when the assassination took place. When my dear papa was shot, his blood covered my uncle and uncle thought they would shoot him too but with God's grace he was spared.

He told me father didn't die quickly and as I write this today, I am crying. This crying, I have done repeatedly for 34 years. This story is difficult to tell but I must tell it.

He was assassinated on Loluai bridge and his body was thrown into the river. He was in the water until, he was retrieved by a kind man and his son downstream and they buried him on the banks of the river.

My father's people – his tribal clan got together and everyone was told to return to the village and receive my father and his two cousin brothers. People from Oria and Paghui villages, brave men mobilised – young and old, and got prepared to go to the temporary graves, and bring my father and his cousins to their land and give them a proper burial.

I pay my respect to my uncles, who were buried on their land at the hamlet down the Oria highway.

Before my father's body was retrieved from the makeshift grave, his people constructed a coffin, a canvas and instructed mother and me to gather blankets and towels to wrap his body.

We went to our special shed that father had built for us before he left for Rabaul. Mother opened the chain lock and we got towels and blankets, with the help of my aunties. I pulled out my doona, which was in its own special zipped cover bag and took it with me.

I gave the doona to my uncle Paue (RIP), and told him to cover my beloved father with it and bring him to a proper burial.

There was a large group of people from both villages, Oria and Paghui, plus hamlets along the highway, who mobilised in vehicles and drove to locations beyond the Loluai river to retrieve the bodies.

We waited for the casket and the lamentations continued, as we waited and waited. My father's people had left before the first light and still hadn't returned and it was past lunch time.

Then we heard wailing before the vehicle came into view. The sight of my father's coffin, brought me to a rain water trough, that had gathered into a makeshift home for frogs. I fell head first into it and in torment laid there, rolling around in mad frenzy.

No words or tears came out. My eyes were locked, I couldn't hear anything, no one existed. My father's kin stopped beside me and laid the coffin on the road, that my father drove his vehicles on. I crawled over and grabbed the edge of the coffin and stayed like that.

My people let me stay and held on, for some time.

As I ran my figures along the wooden coffin, I felt something soft against the wood and when I opened my eyes, I saw part of the doona nailed against the edge and I sobbed the loudest in brokenness.

Before my father's body was retrieved, his people – kin had already dug a grave, in our cemetery just a short distance from our house, where his brother and sister were buried.

When my father's kin went to the makeshift grave along the Loluai river, they dug it out and his two clansmen - two old men whom I respect deeply, may they rest in peace- Pekupei and Ropinau – lifted him out of the temporary grave and placed him into the coffin amongst the blankets. I respect all his people, my people who risked their lives, went to strange lands out of our boundary, dug the grave and got my beloved father. I also pay respect to the man and his son, who pulled out my father's body from Loluai River.

My father's nephew, Pastor Foksy, was a young pastor then. He did a short service at the grave side, while my aunty Otu (RIP) held me, as I lay on the moist soil, both my hands over the hole, with the damp soil on my lips. Otu held me and waited, until my hands were not hanging anymore but lying on the leveled soil, with my father finally buried on his land.

My father was buried FINALLY on his land. May he rest in peace, until that golden day, "For the Lord himself shall descend from heaven with a shout, with the voice of the archangel, and with the trumpet call of God: and the dead in Christ shall rise first (1Thessalonians 4:16).

May God be our only Judge.

The End

Saved by a black angel

By Marlene Dee Gray Potoura
Dedicated to my grandfather (kako) Kauva Moini

WORLD War II came to the Pacific Islands when Moini was working as a policeboy in the highlands of Papua New Guinea, Moini was physically able, a tall and muscular man, and the Australian Army recruited him along with many other fit Papua New Guineans. They were given shotguns and sent out on patrol with the Australian soldiers in the rugged terrain of the highlands.

One morning, Moini's platoon came under Japanese fire as it crossed a one log bridge over a fast-flowing river.

Some men died before they even hit the water and others who jumped met a terrible death against the sharp stones of the river.

Moini felt the log slipping and rode it down to the water. Holding on to the log he allowed the river to sweep him downstream.

After struggling against the torrent, he grabbed a root that had grown into the river and hauled himself to safety. Luckily his shotgun was still belted to his back. Moini rested for a while then sat up and scanned the river and the bank for his mates.

He realised he was alone, and decided to move on as the thick mountain fog was beginning to creep through the trees.

Moini trudged on although tired, cold and hungry. The jungle sounds were unfamiliar and he felt there were Japanese lurking everywhere.

As the night passed and dawn neared, he paused to stand under some trees. He thought of home. He had heard the Australians say that Bougainville and the Solomons were infested by the Japanese.

He wondered how his people were. These thoughts preoccupied him until the darkness thinned and the sounds of morning birds and insects started to come alive.

Moini began walking again. The terrain was still rugged but the trees were shorter. Then, as the new day dawned; the bush gave away to a small village.

He crept silently forward, hidden by some banana trees. There were four round houses. But no one was around. The village was deserted. The people had fled. They'd even left some firewood in one of the houses.

He pulled down a bunch of ripe bananas and slung two more over the barrel of his gun and kept walking. He needed to get back to camp and tell the CO about what had happened to his comrades.

In the distance he could hear a rumble. Another rapid mountain river, he thought. The jungle thickened overhead. The trees were ancient and tall but the floor of the forest was unbelievably clean. The stillness sent goose bumps down his spine.

Then Moini saw a man. He was walking ahead of him and naked. He hadn't seen Moini.

Moini sneaked up silently behind the man, who kept walking very slowly, trying carefully not to fall. Moini pointed the shotgun at him and shouted, "*Yu husat?*" (Who are you?).

The man fell to the ground. Realising the man had fainted, Moini lifted him and saw his face. A foreigner. Japanese? No, he was tall and had fair hair. Must be Australian. Moini stood in confusion, not sure what to do.

He decided to carry the man back to the deserted village. The man was now conscious but too weak to open his eyes.

Moini was hit with the smell of rotting flesh. The poor foreigner had sores all over his body. Big ulcers with white wobbly worms.

Moini struggled to the deserted village and lay the man on some leaves in the round house with the firewood. He lit a fire, rubbing two dry sticks together and ran to a nearby creek to fetch water in a bamboo tube.

He splashed water on the foreigner's face. The man sat up and drank. Then he ate a banana. He was starving, Moini observed silently.

Moini then dried some banana leaves over the fire and pulled the worms from the man's sores.

The hut was now warm and the foreigner watched as Moini moved about blowing the fire and cooking some *kaukau* (sweet potatoes) he'd found.

The foreigner felt safe and thanked God for this unbelievable twist of fate.

He felt an unusual pull towards this man. A black giant, but so gentle with his touch. Who was he?

A sweet thought came into the foreigner's head. He remembered stories from Sunday school. He cleared his throat and Moini looked at him and smiled.

"Are you a black angel?" the foreigner asked, surprised at the sound of his own voice.

"Yes, sir, Lieutenant Carter, sir!" the black man said.

Lieutenant Carter touched his dog tag.

"Can you read, black angel?" Lieutenant Carter asked.

"Yes, sir, I went to a mission school. Taught by white missionaries, sir!"

"Is this your village?"

"No sir, I am from Bougainville, sir!"

"How did you find me?"

"I was with Australian soldiers on patrol, ambushed by the Japs and swept away by the river, sir!"

"Are you the only survivor?"

"I think so, Lieutenant sir!"

There was silence.

"Brother, thank you for saving my life."

"No worries, sir!"

The Lieutenant was sure God had sent this giant black man to save him. He closed his eyes and said a prayer his grandmother taught him.

Truly, this man was an angel in disguise

The tears of an orphan

By Marlene Dee Gray Potoura

Dedicated to my father, Nehemiah Gray Potoura.
Do not judge others. God is our only Judge.

Kuriu was still a baby when his father died during World War 2. He lived with his mother until he was five years old and on his sixth birthday, she left him with her brother Piri and went off to marry a man from the mountain villages.

For seven years, Kuriu lived with his uncle Piri and aunty Laasi. They were barren.

And it was just unfair indeed that uncle Piri was blind and they were very poor.

Kuriu's clothes were rags, old clothes thrown away by the village people that he collected stuck between the stones in the river Leuta, where he went goggle fishing. Kuriu dried them on the rocks and wore them for weeks until they rotted on his ebony skin.

Kuriu always helped uncle Piri work in the gardens. He climbed coconuts when his uncle and aunty asked him to. He went spear fishing in the rivers and always brought home a good catch. He helped aunty Laasi cooked each day and washed their pot and aluminum plates among all the girls down the river, in the main wash area.

All the village boys laughed at him and called him names. They snickered at him when he held his uncle's hand guiding him down to the river. They called him names when he helped carry his aunt's produce from the garden to the market. They wrinkled their noses and laughed loudly at him when he went to school in his tattered clothes.

Heka and Joki always kicked his skinny legs instead of the soccer ball. But Kuriu was a good-natured boy. He was friendly, kind and most of all, honest.

The villagers came to know how unique Kuriu was, after a particular incident.

It all started one morning on a bright and beautiful day. Kuriu, Heka, Joki and some village boys were going fishing at river Pelisa. On their way they went past a watermelon garden. There were big juicy watermelons on every side of the garden. The boys' swallowed hard, thinking of the juicy watermelons.

"Wish I could eat one of those juicy melons," Kuriu laughed, good naturedly as usual.

"Yeah, you're thinking of stealing one, because you are always eating *kaukaus* [sweet potatoes] and your stomach is hard like a stone," Heka laughed sarcastically, followed by loud yodelling from all the boys.

They went on to the river Pelisa and enjoyed themselves. Kuriu speared many fish and shared them with Heka and Joki because they both speared none. When Kuriu got home he helped his aunty to cook the fish and the three of them had a hearty meal.

As his uncle ate the fish and drank the hot creamy soup, he spoke words of appreciation to Kuriu. "My nephew, I am a blind man without children. You are a child of blessing that any parents would want. Your aunty and I are blessed by your heart. I am poor and handicapped, but I swear that your good heart will lead you to be a great man in the future."

His uncle's glassy eyes looked up at the ceiling as he spoke and Kuriu swore in his heart that he would care for this man no matter what. He was never ashamed of being a blind man's nephew.

Early the next morning the garamut sound woke everyone. The village elder yodelled for all families to gather at the football field.

Kuriu led his uncle, with his aunty following closely behind, all went to the football field. Many villagers were there, whispering and murmuring. The chief stood up and cleared his throat.

Silence followed.

"My good people, we have gathered here today because Masiu has requested this meeting. I will now ask Masiu to come forward and talk to us".

Masiu came forward looking very angry. His hands were shaking and his eyes were wild. Everyone knew Masiu. He was a no-nonsense man.

"Yesterday afternoon, I went to my water melon garden and found out that two of my prize watermelons were missing, taken out by thieves. My nephew Heka told me that he went fishing with a couple of village boys. I know now that one of them took the watermelons. I want all the boys who were with Heka yesterday to come up to the front and stand in a straight line," he demanded, looking evilly at Kuriu.

Uncle Piri smiled and let go of Kuriu's hand.

"Stupid old man. Must have taken the watermelons as he sleepwalked last night," uncle Piri laughed loudly at his own joke.

All the boys lined up in front with Kuriu standing last on the line.

Masiu slowly walked in front of the boys, frowning at each of them.

"Ambi, did you steal the watermelons from my garden?" Masiu barked at Ambi who shifted from one foot to another, shaking.

"No I didn't," Ambi whispered fearfully.

"Makui, did you steal the watermelons?" Masiu yelled.

"No, I did not," Makui snapped loudly staring at Masiu.

Kuriu saw Joku and Heka whispering to each other.

"Sania, did you steal the watermelons?" Masiu yelled again.

"No Masiu," Sania answered.

"Joku, did you steal the watermelons?" Masiu yelled one more time

"Masiu, Kuriu stole your watermelons," Joku turned to the villagers as he spoke.

"Yesterday as we walked by the garden, Kuriu told us that he wanted to eat the watermelons. He said his stomach was hard like a stone from eating too many kaukaus and he wanted to eat watermelons to soften it," Joku continued as everyone laughed.

"No, I didn't take any watermelon," Kuriu retorted softly.

"Yes you did, you good for nothing orphan!" Masiu screamed fiercely.

"Hey, stop shouting at my nephew, you sleepwalker!" uncle Piri hollered waving his walking stick in the air.

"Blind man, you cannot see so don't speak," Masiu challenged back.

"Why you good for nothing...." Uncle Piri came forward with his walking stick but the village chief held him back.

"Watermelon thief!" a voice yelled from the crowd.

"Motherless vagrant!" a woman's voice called out.

"Go eat your *kaukaus*, you good for nothing waif."

"Useless fatherless penniless......"

Kuriu bowed his head as the tears flowed from his eyes and fell onto his mud-caked feet. His ears buzzed making him dizzy, as the accusations, hateful words and just overall unkindness flowed from all the men and women, whose children he was friends with and played with every day.

He felt a tightening in his chest and he curled his fingers into a fist, lifted his head up and looked into the clouds and cried in his heart, "Why? why? Forgive me God, if I have done you wrong to deserve this. Forgive me."

As he cried he felt a hand on his arm. He turned around and saw his Aunty Laasi. She pulled his hand kindly and led him to his Uncle Piri, who was waving his walking stick in the air and challenging Masiu and Heka's parents. The village chief stood in between them as he tried to calm everyone down.

"I tell you all. My nephew is the most honest boy this sorry village has and yet you sleepwalker accuses him of something unknown to his character. Come here and let's sort this out, man to man eh. Leave my nephew alone!" Uncle Piri screamed and glared with glazed eyes at everyone in madness. He was beyond reasoning.

"Pay for the watermelons, you skinny orphan," Masiu's wife came forward and yelled at Kuriu, as he was led away by his aunty.

"You want money for your watermelons! You will get it, woman!" aunty Laasi retorted.

When they reached their old broken-down house, uncle Piri took out his most treasured possession: the old metal box with the rusted lock, that had been given to him by an American Bible translator many years back. He waved his walking stick about and fished from under the hearth a weird looking piece of metal, as long as a one-inch nail. He pushed it into the little hollow on the metal box and the box clicked open. Then he pulled out one-kina coins threaded onto a twine. He counted out twenty kina and gave them to Laasi.

"Wife, go and give these to Masiu."

Kuriu thought he saw tears in his sad eyes and he felt an overwhelming love for his blind uncle.

Very early in the morning the next day, there was a different kind of commotion. A woman was wailing and moaning in sheer madness. All the village women folk ran to comfort her. Laasi and Kuriu ran outside to see what was happening.

"Goodness, it's Heka's mother," she said as she ran to join the other women.

Kuriu and his uncle waited in their house. A short while later she returned with the news of the commotion.

"Piri," she gasped fearfully. "Heka's stomach has tripled in size overnight and it is still swelling. Something is wrong with that boy."

A pastor was called to come and pray for Heka. In front of all the village people, he asked Heka if there was anything he wanted to say, before a prayer would be offered.

Heka started crying and then he said, "I ate the two watermelons and I am sorry."

There was complete silence.

Then the old village chief announced in a serious tone of voice.

"Before the pastor prays, I would like to ask all those who have accused Kuriu of theft to come forward shake his hand, give him two kina and say sorry to him".

Everyone came forward and shook Kuriu's hand and gave him K2.00. Kuriu shook their hands, nodded his head kindly and smiled at each of them.

After the pastor had offered a prayer on Heka's behalf, the village people slowly walked to their homes.

Later in the afternoon a miracle occurred – a miracle that no one had the courage to open their mouths to explain or even discuss.

Heka started heaving and his stomach tightened like a tidal wave about to surge. He opened his mouth and screamed as he spurted nothing but the crimson watery remains of what he had stolen and eaten. As he vomited, his stomach went back to its normal size and he sat up for the first time after laying down the whole day with a swollen, balloon-like stomach.

Heka stood up and ran to Kuriu's house and said sorry for all that he had caused. Kuriu, as good-natured as ever, accepted the apology and shook his friend's outstretched hands.

This is a lesson to all boys and girls: that outward appearances do not count. It is the heart that matters. A good heart is a winner, no matter what.

Glossary

Ahoto - women carry ahotos on their backs.

Aibia - name of river

Apili breakfast food – cooked banana mashed with grated coconut

Arakamo - spirit fire that moves at night

Aului- thatched hut used for cooking

Aupa kumus - edible green vegetable

BougAir – Bougainville Airlines

Bubu – General term for grandma or grandpa

Cessna – airplanes for BougAir

Choko tips – edible greens

Galip nuts – tropical nuts, from the galip tree

Hauskuk - kitchen

Hurinampo – traditional green vegetable from Warabung, EHP

Irinioku – Area School for Adventist students in South Bougainville.

Kako – matrilineal grandfather

Kangu wharf – wharf in South Bougainville

Karapa – metre tall wild grass, distressingly difficult to get rid of.

Kariani – traditional mat

Kava/tamatama – mashed banana in coconut cream, heated over fire.

Kominis – common vine that grows over grass.

Kuipanana – dark witch

Kurupaho – epileptic

Kutuke – cave ghoul

Laplap - sarong

Levolevo – slim one and a half metre traditional axe.

Loutoi – covered in leaves and buried in hot ashes to cook.

Mamo – patrilineal grandmother

Mandai tree – wild palm tree

Maraham – edible ferns that grow in humid places.

Mareua/mareuwa – edible leaves from the Tulip tree(Tok-pisin).

Masimasi – mashed taro with galip nuts (Traditional food)

Moileu – Mother tree

Moloana – Name of river in Irinioku

Mouroru – Clearing in front of house or in-between where people gather.

Mumu – to cook food with heated stones covered in leaves

Nono – patrilineal grandfather or father's uncle, the female child can address him as nono.

Nonambaro – village in the Daulo district.

Okilo – Rosewood tree

Pauhu – River in Oria

Pingping – smooth stone for cracking galip nuts

Pirasi – name of river

Pisokokui – small hamlet in Oria

Pohurai – witchcraft or someone who poisons other people through food, water and food scraps

Porutoro- unique delicious yam in Oria

Pukai – traditional bag carried by men in Oria

Pumpkin tips – edible greens

Rekai – tradition greens from Watabung, Daulo, EHP

Scrapped tapiok – Tapiok tuber that has been scrapped.

Soro- Vast forest land belong to Potoura clan

Tapiok/tapioca – root vegetable

Taraha - name of creek

Tava – woven with bamboo and hung over fireplace for smoking meat and other food.

Teite – matrilineal grandmother

Tomba – seat made of wood

Tomea – delicious green cooking banana in Oria

Torohuis – traditional tattoo markings on face, slit with fine bamboo.

Torre – flooring made with mandai palms

Tuha – tiniest fire ant

Turau – name of coastal land and beach area

Wuhuva – traditional like basil leaves used for flavouring food in Oria.

Wuloli – Bubbling creek.

My mama, Margaret Potoura (Photo credit: Linda Potoura)

My cousin Nehemiah with his young family.

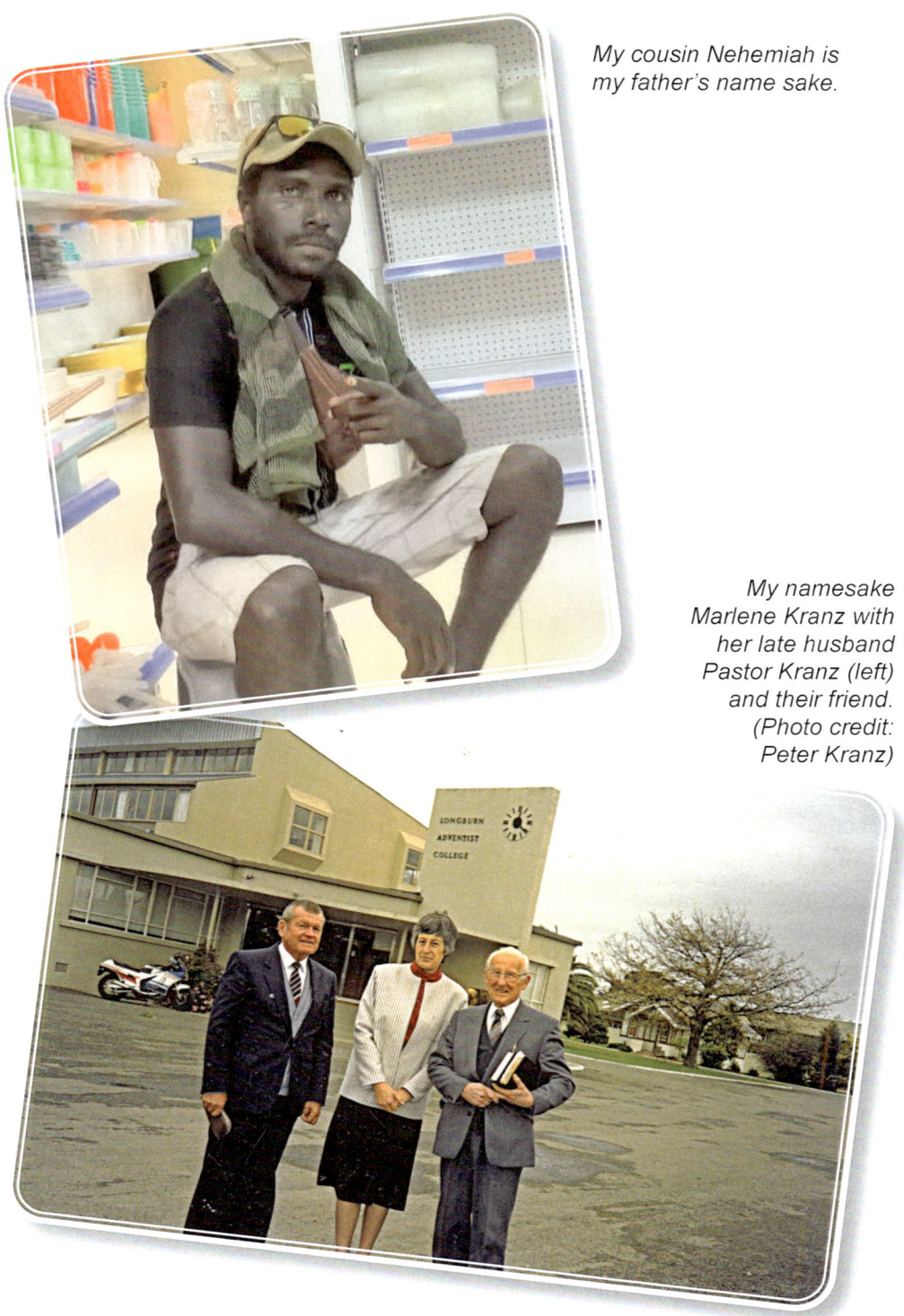

My cousin Nehemiah is my father's name sake.

My namesake Marlene Kranz with her late husband Pastor Kranz (left) and their friend. (Photo credit: Peter Kranz)

I teach English at Paradise College, these days.

With some of my grade 11 students after our drama performance at Moresby Arts Theatre (2021) Paradise College

www.ingramcontent.com/pod-product-compliance
Lightning Source LLC
Chambersburg PA
CBRC091957300426
44109CB00007BA/159